GROWING UP POOR AND LUCKY IN NEW YORK CITY

Praise for Growing Up Poor and Lucky in New York City

Tom Herbert entertains with stories of 1960s adolescent culture in vibrant, colorful Ozone Park. His descriptions of neighborhood characters, family, and friends do not disappoint. A great addition to memoirs about that era in New York history.

– James M. O'Kane, PhD
Professor Emeritus, Sociology
Drew University, Madison, NJ

With amazing clarity Tom recalls his early years living like a kid in the world's craziest candy store, Brooklyn and Queens. The fights, the schemes, the plans, the dreams, it's all here. A wonderfully hilarious and touching memoir.

– Daniel Elisii
The Lahaska Bookshop

GROWING UP POOR AND LUCKY IN NEW YORK CITY

A Brooklyn/Queens Success Story

Tom Herbert

GROWING UP POOR AND LUCKY IN NEW YORK CITY
A Brooklyn/Queens Success Story

Copyright © 2019 Thomas Herbert

ISBN 978-0-578-60400-8

On the cover: 910 Hancock Street, Brooklyn, Tom Herbert's first home as a child. (Photo by Tom Herbert)

*For my beautiful wife
Carmela, the main reason
I grew up so lucky.*

Herbert Family Crest

CONTENTS

Author's Note

This story is based on true events. However, it is a work of creative nonfiction and is my version of the truth. Certain names have been changed. In certain instances, dialogue has been reconstructed based on my memories. Some might have different memories or interpretations of this story.

GROWING UP POOR AND LUCKY IN NEW YORK CITY

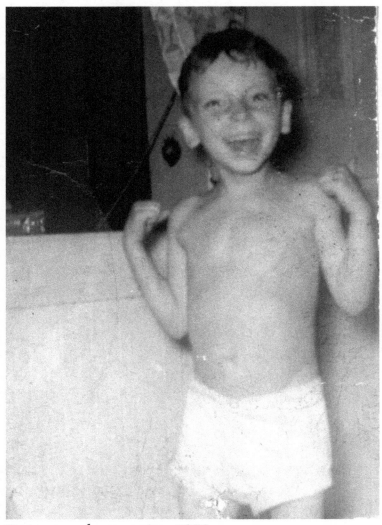

Young muscle-man, circa 1956.

CHAPTER ONE

BUSHWICK TO SOUTH OZONE PARK

1952-1962

When I was born in July 1952, most likely as an accident and surprise, my parents' marriage was already on the rocks. My father worked at the Brooklyn Navy Yard as a burner/welder, earning perhaps a hundred bucks a week with overtime. Mom volunteered at the Our Lady of Good Counsel rectory. I always thought of my family as middle class. In truth, we were pretty poor.

But I considered myself a lucky child. I got to live the first ten years of my life in the Bushwick section of Brooklyn. The neighborhood changed around us–and not for the better. We moved three times before I was ten, always into six-family apartment buildings. Odds were bad the five other families in any building were sane, clean, or even neighborly. One neighbor's dog once chased and dragged me down the front stoop. I was bitten and taken to Unity Hospital. Our neighbors knew the dog was healthy, though, so I avoided a very painful anti-rabies injection.

On another occasion, as we ate dinner and watched the Three Stooges and Officer Joe Bolton on TV, our new Italian neighbors in the next apartment screamed and cursed. Brute Bernard and Skull Murphy would have envied their wrestling match. Finally, they both burst through our kitchen door. Our dog, Queenie, jumped up and bit the fat wife on the ass. My father, who wasn't a big guy but had very strong arms, picked up the husband and threw him out the door and against the wall in the corridor. We never heard from them again. Just another relaxing dinner in Bushwick.

Each of our apartment buildings was a little more rundown than the previous one. Many were built in the 1910s and 1920s following the 1908 construction of the subway connection over the Williamsburg Bridge. By the 1950s and 1960s, they showed their years of neglect. Fuses were often blown because there wasn't ample capacity to service six families.

The Bushwick apartments were railroad-style with five or six rooms lined up in a straight row from the front bedroom overlooking Hancock Street to the rear fire escape adjoining the kitchen. The apartments were cleverly designed so the bathtub was tucked away in a closet-like corner in the first bedroom. There were no showers and only one small toilet with an overhead water tank. We pulled a chain with a wooden handle to flush.

Each building had an assigned "super" entrusted with maintaining the apartments. He took out the trash and kept the heat working. There was no air conditioning. Lucky tenants had a fan or two in their apartment.

We lived with hundreds of roaches. It was always scary to come home at night, turn on the kitchen light, and watch them scurry away. My mother always kept our apartment well cleaned, but if the apartments around us weren't, the roaches moved right in. Bug spray was effective for about ten minutes. If one tenant hired an exterminator, the roaches simply moved to an adjoining apartment until the unpleasant odor diminished.

We got accustomed to them, but the beetle-like water bugs made me nervous. They were ten times larger than roaches–almost the size of my thumb. When I got out of bed at night and accidentally stepped on one, they made a cool squishy sound.

There were mice, and reportedly rats, living in the basement where the storage bins for our trash were kept. I was afraid to go down there. I always suspected lazy neighbors were responsible for the roaches and rodents. Rather than use the steel cans by the fences in front of the tenements, some threw their garbage out the window. Other tossed bags of it down the cellar stairs.

During the day and in the summer months, the streets were relatively safe. We played stickball on side streets, allowing for car traffic. We roller skated. We played marbles and skelsy, also known as skelly, with a chalk-outlined board in the middle of the street. We flicked wax-filled bottle caps with our thumbs, trying to land them in a series of numbered boxes. The game was a great way to fine-tune our competitive spirit though it was rough on the fingernails. I left the house in the morning and didn't come back until my mother leaned out the third-floor window and announced dinner.

My mother was a stylish housewife standing 5 feet even. One could imagine she was extremely attractive as a young adult. Being the baby of the family, I spent time alone with her while my siblings were at school. She was kind, attentive, and direct in her parenting. She wasn't strict, but I knew she wouldn't put up with any monkey business. When she called me in for dinner, I went quickly.

Tom's beautiful mom, Marie, circa 1940s.

We rarely had a dull moment. Between the street gangs in Bushwick, both black and white, and the nuts living in the apartment buildings, a palpable sense of genuine danger lurked around every corner. One day a bunch of us were playing tag. We ran in between cars and into the street to avoid being tagged. One of the new Spanish kids, who was "it," chased after another kid to catch him. He never saw the car that ran him over. An ambulance took him away. He never came back.

As the youngest of four children, I had plenty of company at home and tended to look up to my two brothers and sister. My sister, Ginger, short for Virginia, was eight years older than I was. She was close to my mother and a great role model for studying and staying out of trouble. Back then she had a boyfriend, Lorenzo, a Marine who told lots of war stories and was fun to be around when he wasn't deployed somewhere. Eventually they broke up.

My brother Danny was three years older than Ginger and quite a character. He hid in the dark, dingy hallways of our apartment buildings and jumped from the shadows to scare the crap out of me. To get even, I put pots and pans under his sheets. When he attempted to sneak in from Benny's Tavern, where he wasn't supposed to be, and jumped into his bed, the pots and pans crashed, making him curse loudly. The ruckus woke the entire house. Loved it!

My oldest brother, Victor, the apple of my mother's eye, was bright, good looking, focused, and studious. He had a vocation to become a Catholic priest, which pleased my fairly religious mother. Members of various religious orders were involved with our family, including Father Francis McCabe, who, I suspect, guided Victor toward the priesthood. He visited the apartment on holidays and brought gifts for me and my siblings from time to time. My parents named me Thomas Francis after my Uncle Tom, a New York City firefighter, and Father McCabe.

Having Victor around was always special. Since his religious aspirations didn't allow him to date, he sometimes took me to the movies or into the city. Other times he played ball in the streets with me and my friends. Victor could make a game out of anything. He once tried to smuggle me on an Eastern Airlines flight to Puerto Rico as a standby seminarian. He wore his seminarian outfit, complete with a priestly collar, and had me dress similarly. We must have looked funny to the airline people, sort of like Austin Powers and Mini-Me, since I was only ten years old and clearly not a seminarian or priest. We didn't get on that flight. Many standby passengers were ahead of us. We just went home, but it was worth the try.

One benefit of Victor becoming a priest was a free educational ride. College tuition was a challenge for our family. How great that the Diocese of Brooklyn paid for his education. We were all very proud of Victor for his commitment to a higher calling. There was one catch–the enormous amount of dedication and sacrifice it takes to become a priest. He was basically sequestered in Immaculate Conception Seminary in Huntington, Long Island. He was rarely allowed visitors, either. Since we didn't own a car, we couldn't easily get there, anyway.

Victor came home for the Thanksgiving and Christmas holidays, which was a high point for the family. Sometimes we asked friends or neighbors to drive us out to pick up Victor or drop him off after the holidays. When the owner of a local candy store drove us one time, he almost crashed on the treacherous Interboro Parkway. The arrangements weren't easy for anybody, but it was certainly an adventure.

Our last address in Bushwick was on Evergreen Avenue, where we'd lived in several tenements. Well-informed sources told me we moved every other year because my father didn't pay the rent on time. When I was ten my family moved to South Ozone Park in another borough, Queens. There was still never enough money.

My father bought a used car from a friend at the Brooklyn Navy Yard. Though several years old, it was serviceable. In a rare moment of family harmony one day, my father suggested that my mom and I hop in the car and take a drive to Rockaway Beach. I'd been there once before and remembered the long, wooden boardwalk and the arcades and rides at Rockaway Playland near the beach. I was excited to have a nice evening with Mom and Dad and just me. I sat in the back seat. We rolled down the windows. Warm summer breezes blew gently through the car.

As we cruised east through Howard Beach, we passed the Big Bow Wow and Pizza City restaurants. I secretly hoped we'd stop at Carvel for an ice cream cone. No such luck. We blew right past the last Carvel store before crossing into Broad Channel. The aroma of saltwater and songs of circling seagulls heightened my excitement. We motored down Cross Bay Boulevard and over the water on both sides of the highway. My dad slowed the car just before the final bridge, which connected Broad Channel to the Rockaway peninsula. He turned around and headed back to Bushwick. No rides. No Skee-Ball. No nothing. There was a problem–the ten-cent toll before the bridge to Rockaway. My father didn't have a dime.

Somehow, though, we'd thought life in South Ozone Park would be better. It wasn't that far from where we used to live. Along its western boundary, Queens borders Brooklyn. The Queens neighborhoods of Woodhaven and Richmond Hill adjoin at Atlantic Avenue to the north and South Conduit Avenue to the south.

The southern section of Queens, closer to JFK airport, was once rich with corner bars, pizza joints, luncheonettes, and delicatessens. In addition to a large Italian American population, South Ozone Park also had its share of Irish, Germans, Polish, French, and Jewish people back in the 1960s. The developers who built the snug cookie-cutter houses that line the sequentially numbered streets in southern Queens came up with the word "Ozone." They wanted to entice prospective home buyers with the romance of fragrant ozone-like sea breezes drifting north from the not-too-distant beaches of the nearby Atlantic Ocean.

The park-like community was created in the late 1880s. It saw tremendous population growth in the 1920s when most of the homes were constructed. The boom was fueled by easy access on the Fulton Street elevated subway line, which ran along Liberty Avenue. Working people could get to Manhattan or Brooklyn for a nickel each way. The population rose from forty thousand to more than one hundred thousand people between 1914 when the elevated line was completed and 1930 when the infamous John Adams High School was erected. Perhaps back then there were fragrant beach-like breezes in the air.

Over the years the blue-collar neighborhood grew even more. Families wanted the "country life" with trees and lawns on their sprawling 20′x 40′lots. In the 1960s many of these homes sold for ten to fifteen thousand dollars. We bought ours on 115th Street, just off Rockaway Boulevard, in the early 1960s. By the time we arrived, South Ozone Park smelled like jet fuel from nearby Idlewild Airport, horse manure from the Big A (Aqueduct Racetrack) a few blocks away, and putrid "ozone" from the dump called Jamaica Bay. On a damp, hot, breezy summer day, the air was thick enough to see almost three houses away.

While somewhat diverse, our neighborhood was primarily Catholic. The two closest Catholic elementary schools were St. Anthony's and Our Lady of Perpetual Help. Both were packed to capacity and run by nuns who ruled with intimidation and brute force. Class sizes were maxed out. Many residents couldn't abide the idea of sending their children to one of the public schools, P.S. 100 or P.S. 108. It was out of the question.

Tuition at the Catholic schools was relatively cheap, after all, and few parents wanted their little angels to wind up in John Adams, where it was easier to get drugs than an education. Around that time John Adams was selected as an "integration" site–an effort to racially balance the quality of education. Students from minority areas, including South Jamaica and Baisley Park, were put on buses and mixed into what had been almost exclusively white classrooms. I never attended John Adams, but friends told terrifying stories of fights and riots in and around the cafeteria and in the schoolyard. Many kids just cut classes, they said, since there wasn't a lot of learning going on, anyway.

Chapter Two

The Glue that Never Stuck

1965 - 1969

I could walk or ride my bike from my house on 115th Street and Rockaway Boulevard to four or five candy stores. During the 1960s and 1970s these establishments, also part luncheonette, were headquarters for many teens whose parents preferred them out of the house but in the neighborhood. Typically, these stores were owned and operated by immigrant families who lived behind or above them. Some of these hard-working and incredibly patient storeowners were Holocaust survivors with ID numbers tattooed on their wrists.

Lilly's, between 115th and 116th streets on the Boulevard, featured an excellent assortment of penny candies, fountain drinks, newspapers, cigarettes, and ice cream sold by the pint, quart, or scoop. Breyers was the leading brand in Queens at that time. Lilly and her husband, Ira, had two twin sons, Simon and Eli. They all lived behind a curtain in the rear of the store.

Lilly's was not the cleanest store in the neighborhood. One hot summer day pavement ants overran the place and occupied the lower candy shelves, including but not limited to the Tootsie Rolls and Raisinets. People were aghast! Adults, that is. We kids kept buying the penny and nickel candy, brushing the little creatures off, and kissing the candy up to God. The treats melted in our mouths.

Closer to the Aqueduct Racetrack on 114th Street and Rockaway Boulevard was Anna's candy store and luncheonette. Anna's had the usual assortment of daily necessities plus hot dogs for twenty-five cents apiece and an outstanding fifty-cent meatball sandwich. It was a storefront or two away from a couple of taverns or, as we called them, gin mills. Menacing-looking loan sharks and wise guys frequented that corner. The word on the street was you could get a pack of Marlboro's and an egg cream and play the numbers at Anna's for $1.85 without leaving the slightly worn-out counter stools, which occupied about 85 percent of the store.

Bambi's on Lefferts and 135th Avenue in my neighborhood was yet another option. Yes, they offered a full line of newspapers, including the *Daily News*, the *Post*, the *Long Island Press*, *Journal American* and, of course, the *Mirror*. They also sold cigarettes, Italian ices, potato chips, and all you would expect to find in a Queens candy store, but they excelled at magazines.

One of my friends, Alfred, also an altar boy at our local Catholic church, was famous for knowing exactly what time and day Bambi's would get the latest issue of *Playboy*. Al arrived shortly after the magazines were placed on the display rack. He casually approached and flipped through *Mad*, *Life*, and sometimes *Look* magazines before purposely dropping two issues of *Playboy* on the floor. Slyly sliding one under his shirt while returning the other to the shelf, Al was on his way to masturbation glory. That Al had nerves of steel. His remarkable courage probably was steadied by the wine he drank before and after serving Mass.

All these stores were interesting and remarkable. None was as well-known, though, as the one on Lefferts and Sutter (L&S), owned first by Izzy and Ethel but eventually acquired by the notorious Sam and Helen. All four were Holocaust survivors. These hard-working immigrants had been through hell during the World War II years. Why did they put up with a never-ending stream of rowdy kids and teenagers that hung out in front of, around, inside, and occasionally on top of their store? It's a mystery.

Stealing was ongoing but rose to the status of an art form at Sam and Helen's. While some kids sat at the counter slurping egg creams, lime rickeys, and Mountain Dew, others rifled the magazine racks. Sam, who had a perpetually runny nose, bent down to scoop ice cream for a malted or ice cream float and wiped his large, unsightly nose, never 100 percent successfully. As droplets of who-knows-what crowned those scoops, other kids pocketed corn cob pipes and rolling paper from the other side of the store.

Glue sniffing was a popular and affordable activity for some of our gang, too. The glue-sniffing and Carbona-huffing gang eventually ran into a serious problem. Sam and Helen became suspicious when several guys bought airplane glue every night without also purchasing the plastic airplane and car models that went with it. Naturally, the profit was in the models, not the glue.

So Sam and Helen announced a new policy: you could no longer buy a tube of glue unless you bought a toy model to go with it. There was panic in the streets! First, who had enough money to buy an airplane model? One could cost two or three bucks. Second, the store carried a limited supply of plastic model inventory. We needed a fund-raising solution. One of the gang came up with a great idea. In the rear of the store was a phone booth used by bookies to place bets, boys to call girls, girls to call boys, boys and girls to make out, and husbands to call other guys' wives.

Mooch, who had an early interest in telecommunications, jammed up the coin return slot in the phone with napkins so no one got their change. Each evening Mooch removed the jammed paper napkin with a paper clip designed to clear the slot. He made that phone into a slot machine that always paid off. Naturally, the passive income was used to fund supplies, corn cob pipes, and cigarettes for the gang.

Mooch also figured out how to make free phone calls. He inserted foil from a pack of gum or cigarettes into the coin slot, faking the phone into thinking it was money. Very clever, that Mooch.

At some point during the summer of 1966, the candy store ran out of airplane and car models. This had little to do with the building of models and everything to do with the sniffing/huffing of glue. As new models came into stock, they sold out almost immediately. What was the glue-sniffing community to do for a cheap high?

The solution was **reverse** shoplifting. As soon as a model was purchased, along with a tube or two of Testors best glue, the purchaser slipped the model under his shirt and either returned it to inventory or just recycled the same model and bought it over and over again. The owners were happy. The kids were happy, and the glue manufacturers were thrilled since sales of glue that summer must have increased 100 percent. The system became known as "the glue that never stuck."

Because I had asthma as a child, I found sniffing glue and huffing Carbona distasteful and never participated. I enjoyed watching the antics, though. Occasionally a guy would entice one or two neighborhood girls to join the fun. When he got them high enough, he took advantage of them in the vacant lots near my friend Billy's house or behind the VFW on Sutter and 118th Street. One girl, particularly susceptible to the seduction of inhalants, was a favorite among guys seeking cheap thrills and easy hand releases. For some girls, reputations were hard to protect. Once diminished, they were lost forever. One could say those bad reputations stuck!

CHAPTER THREE

NUNS

1965-1966

E veryone knew John wasn't a great student. In a later era he might have been classified as "learning disabled" or "intellectually challenged." In 1965 at Our Lady of Perpetual Help (OLPH) Catholic Grammar School, he was just considered dumb. He typically scored 40 percent on our weekly spelling tests, which meant he correctly spelled eight of twenty vocabulary words. The failing grade must have embarrassed him since the toughest words on the list were "supermarket" and "automobile."

John, who was Italian American like most of the forty-five students in our class, believed the nuns hated all of us, especially him. As far as we could tell, like myself, most of the OLPH nuns were of Irish descent, at least from what little we could see of them in their flying nun habits.

Sister Denise, our eighth-grade teacher, was a sadistic, seemingly frustrated woman in her late fifties. She was mean and ran her classroom with an iron fist, as did many Dominican sisters of that era. She was a slapper who occasionally used a yardstick as a weapon but could also chuck an eraser faster and more accurately than Sandy Koufax.

While never shy about physically abusing me or my classmates, her specialty was public humiliation. She made comedian Don Rickles seem like a nice guy. It was bad enough to get slapped across the face for talking during class or looking out the window. Sister Denise also made us stand in front of the room and called us names like "loser," "imbecile," and "moron." All in the name of God, of course.

During one such verbal assault on John, who'd been caught chewing gum or some other near-capital offense, Sister Denise met her demise. She summoned John to the front of the room and told him to kneel in front of the blackboard. The good sister's plan was to stick John's chewing gum in his hair–SOP for Dominican nuns. Unable to show their own hair, they seemed obsessed with ruining everybody else's.

John hesitated to kneel, so Sister Denise tried to grab his tie and yank him down. That way he'd be within slapping distance. Little did she know John was wearing a clip-on tie. As she pulled, it popped off, throwing her off-balance and sending her crashing into the chalk ledge at the bottom of the blackboard. She hit her back, yelled an obscenity that sounded a lot like "fudge," and fell to her knees. Silence fell for what seemed like hours. We were all shocked to see Sister Denise on her knees in front of John, who was also on his knees.

The tension broke when John broke into a sinister giggle, prompting Sister Denise to jump up and kick him with her little black nun shoes. Bruce Lee would have been proud. The class broke into cheers and laughter, which further infuriated the good sister and made things worse for John. Sister Denise was out of service for at least a week, which was a week less than the suspension John received. From that day forward, John was our hero. Nobody thought less of him even though he couldn't spell worth a damn.

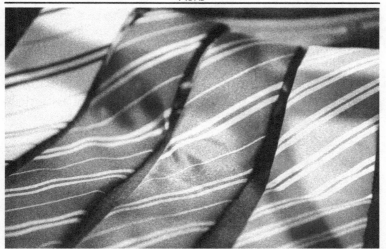

Photo by Rhii Photography on Unsplash

On another occasion Sister Denise left the answer key for a state-required standardized reading test open on her desk. As we all returned from lunch, one of the kids discovered the answer key, naked and available, on top of the teacher's test packets. One of the kids jotted down the multiple-choice answers on the back of his ruler. Others followed his lead.

Just to be cool, I joined the pack and copied down the sequence. I certainly didn't need the answer key. I excelled in reading, spelling, and vocabulary. The answers to a math test would have been much more helpful.

There were at least a dozen kids surrounding that desk when Sister Denise walked in. At first, we startled her. We madly scrambled to our desks. Gradually, she figured out what we were up to. She looked out at the class.

"Who was at my desk?" she demanded, menacingly. "And why?"

Call me naïve or stupid, but I was the only one to stand up and admit it. The little weasel who started it shook in his boots. He never said a word. I incorrectly assumed the other culprits would own up to the crime, too. Surely they wouldn't let me take the fall for everyone. It was bad to cheat. In my brainwashed mind, though, it was worse to lie to a nun.

A swat team of nuns descended on the room. They berated and threatened me, the only honest/dishonest kid in the room. Everyone, including the nun who caught us, knew lots of kids were at that desk. I looked at John and Regis and Marky. No one looked back at me. I faced expulsion and my friends, it seemed, were willing to let me die alone. As the nuns began individual interrogations, someone leaked a name. That kid leaked another. Before long, to my relief, five or six of us were in trouble. As the only guilty party, I would have been an easy target. It'd be a lot harder to expel a half dozen of us. As a punishment we were given a minimal passing grade for Reading that semester. The other half dozen guilty kids got away with it.

That day I learned never to follow a crowd. The nun learned never to leave out the answer key. I wondered, though, if Sister Denise had deliberately left it open on her desk to boost our class performance on the standardized test. Doubtful but possible!

When my class graduated later that year, John wrote in my yearbook: "May your troubles be as far apart as Sister Denise's front teeth." Couldn't have said it better myself.

CHAPTER FOUR

THOM MCAN SHOE STORE CAPER

1967- 1968

I n our neighborhood, crawling with fascinating people, someone occasionally stood out for doing something really creative. Such an event took place in 1967 on Liberty Avenue two blocks from where the A train elevated subway line ended. Liberty Avenue was densely packed with retail stores of every variety–restaurants (none of Michelin quality, I'm afraid), clothing stores, dry cleaners, record stores, candy stores, liquor stores, movie theaters (Lefferts and Casino), a few pizza places (then fifteen cents a slice), and many shoe stores.

One warm summer night at around 10 p.m., an hour after the Thom McAn shoe store closed for business, an idea arose in the somewhat clouded mind of one Freddy O'Neill. Quick to fight and slow to think about consequences, Freddy was someone to avoid at all costs. He was smoking at age twelve and experimenting with alcohol soon thereafter. There was a look about Freddy that gave people the chills. His crooked smile revealed slightly nicotine-stained teeth. His non-GQ attire matched the blank, cloudy look in his eyes. Freddy seemed to wear the same outfit for weeks at a time–a black <u>woolen cap,</u>

baggy blue jeans with a tear around the left knee, and an Army/Navy store sweatshirt that appeared to have been handed down from one of his older twin brothers. He barely attended the local Catholic grammar school and initially found it inconvenient to continue his educational studies at nearby John Adams High School, a cesspool of failure and racial tension.

The unemployed Freddy occasionally shoplifted. He returned soda bottles for the five-cent deposit at the A&P on Rockaway Boulevard. He borrowed change from various sources. It was tough. After all, a quart of Colt 45 Malt Liquor at the local deli cost ninety cents.

According to neighborhood tribal knowledge and lore, he came up with a plan: After closing hours at Thom McAn's, he'd throw a brick through the front window, steal the shoes on display, and sell them to friends and neighbors. Let's face it, the shoes in the window were really nice, as were the small selection of sneakers. Some were leading brands. Freddy found his brick in the lots on 122nd Street off Sutter Avenue. He pedaled his brother's beat-up bike with the newspaper basket the six blocks from Rockaway Boulevard to Liberty Avenue.

Freddy launched his brick just as the nearby A train entered the station. Surely the train would mask the sound of breaking glass. The brick bounced off the store's display window. Twice. On his third try, he succeeded. The window cracked and split into three ragged pieces before giving way enough for Freddy to slide into the display platform. In less than five minutes he stuffed nearly sixty shoes, moccasins, and sneakers into his borrowed laundry bag. Then he was off and pedaling for home as fast as he could, never looking back.

It probably had never occurred to him his target audience was limited to a specific group of handicapped people–people with only one leg. To make things more difficult, people with only a left leg. When Freddy dumped out his stolen shoe collection, he must have discovered what many people already knew: Thom McAn's only displayed left-footed shoes. There wasn't a pair among them.

We lost track of Freddy after the shoe store heist. Some thought he hung out at the greasy diner on Rockaway Boulevard and Lefferts, but nobody knew for sure what happened to him.

Freddy was unique. While there were lots of characters in the neighborhood, few had the creative energy to attempt and carry out an actual heist.

Photo by Nathan Dumlao on Unsplash

CHAPTER FIVE

THE ALTAR BOYS

1964-1968

Being an altar boy at Our Lady of Perpetual Help came with a certain status in 1964. To qualify a boy needed better than average grades, the endorsement of the nun teaching the sixth grade, and the blessing of the principal.

The job had its perks. There was generally plenty of wine available. Some guys liked to gulp down a bit before mass, just to take the edge off. We got out of class to separate the palm in the rectory prior to Palm Sunday. Sometimes we also got to serve a funeral mass or quickie wedding during the week. Funerals were the best because funeral directors sometimes tipped us for assisting with the casket trolley.

There was a pecking order among altar boys. The bottom rank was an acolyte, followed by a senior who was just below a master server. Each had assigned duties during funerals. Master altar boys ran the show. They assisted the priest with wine and water, fetched the Bible, and turned the page to the correct passages for the day, which had to be marked with colorful silk page markers. For many of us the job was a challenge.

Photo by Aaron Burden on Unsplash

For some reason I was selected to be a master altar boy. Father Washa met me in church one rainy Saturday afternoon and did a ten-minute walk-through of my duties. No notes. No YouTube. No nothing. I was clueless. For about three weeks, I lucked out. Each time my altar server team was called for a funeral, the ceremony was a short service rather than a full monty funeral mass. I had the short version down.

One morning, as we arrived at church, we were horrified to learn Father Hein, the meanest priest in the rectory, was assigned to our funeral. It was going to be the big one. The church was packed. Father Hein, who had a very strong German accent, was grumpy and unapproachable on a good day. I thought about mentioning this would be my first attempt at a full funeral mass but chose instead to bluff my way through.

It did not go well. The first problem was that the altar server cards–cue cards with all the necessary prayers, normally placed on the first step of the altar–were missing.

Back then, prior to the Second Vatican Council, priests had their backs to the congregation while celebrating mass. They also spoke in Latin. When I became an altar boy, the required prayers were recited in Latin. I had a rough idea how to say the *Confiteor* but had no chance at all with the *Sucipiat*. I had mastered it when I first signed on but had long since forgotten everything beyond the first two lines. About two sentences in, Father Hein realized I was mumbling like a child with a mouth full of oatmeal. Clearly not impressed, he completed the prayers on my behalf.

As the ceremony progressed and I was supposed to be on his right, I found myself on his left. He gestured me to the right position. When the time came to fetch the lectionary for the readings, I knelt, silently frozen in time. He turned and pointed to the stand holding the Holy Book. I jumped up and brought the Bible to him. It must have been opened to yesterday's news because he impatiently flipped the pages until he found what he needed.

As my face turned redder and redder from embarrassment, his face did likewise out of anger. After the service he approached me.

"What in the world were you trying to do out there?" he asked.

"It was my first full funeral mass," I explained, "and I've barely been trained."

"It will be your last full funeral mass," he said. "You are apparently not trainable."

After that I was relegated to regular server duties. No tips. And whenever I jumbled and slurred my attempts at Latin to bluff through prayers, he winced.

Assigned to serve an evening mass one time, I finished my assignment and was horrified to find someone had stolen my bike right outside the church. Imagine stealing a bike with mass in progress. Worse, imagine stealing it from an altar boy. As we learned in the *Baltimore Catechism*, anyone who steals a bike from an altar boy while he's serving mass would burn in hell. Several years later, I may have spotted someone I didn't know riding that bike. It looked the worse for wear. The person riding it claimed his mother bought it for him for Christmas. Who knows?

One altar boy, the class clown, managed to get past the background check. His name was Bill. He had no moral issues with helping himself to a few hosts before mass and washing them down with altar wine. We were twelve at the time. In the middle of serving a Sunday mass, Bill was fooling around. He grabbed his crotch and tried to make me laugh. I didn't think Father Telly, who was officiating, caught the comedy act. He had.

Without missing a beat he faced the altar, made the sign of the cross, and knocked Bill clear off the first two steps with one blind backhand strike to his face. Acting as if nothing had happened, he continued the mass in record time. After mass he grabbed Bill by his ear and herded him back to the rectory for coaching and counseling. That was Bill's last mass.

I loved serving Sunday masses. I tickled the throats of my friends and a few really pretty girls with the Communion plate. It always brought a smile to their faces.

One summer I must have served mass at least fifty times. I showed up at 6:15 a.m. for the 6:30 a.m. mass. Visiting priests celebrated masses on one of our side altars between the regularly scheduled masses. One actually tipped me for helping him. Another time I served two different masses simultaneously. I thought at the time, *Surely this will take time off my purgatory sentence.*

Somewhere between sixth grade, when I was a holy roller, and seventh grade, when I discovered girls and they discovered me, my life became more complicated. Not necessarily better but definitely more interesting.

Chapter Six

Plane Crashes and Other Disasters

1964-1965

Eastern Airlines Flight 663 originated in Boston. En route to Atlanta, it had a scheduled stopover at JFK Airport on Monday, February 8, 1965. That DC-7 never made it to Atlanta. Sadly, it crashed in New York just after takeoff, killing all seventy-nine passengers and a crew of five.

We lived so close to Kennedy Airport, it was only a short bike ride away. A friend named Harry from Our Lady of Perpetual Help suggested we ride to the crash site on Tuesday, the day following the tragedy. Both of us had *Long Island Press* newspaper routes and sturdy enough bikes to attempt the several-mile journey through some treacherous neighborhoods.

We met at my house on 115th Street after school on February 9 and set out. We made it as far as Baisley Boulevard but decided to turn back due to dark clouds and dark and dirty looks from the locals. We returned safely to South Ozone Park and headed down Sutter Avenue and 118th Street.

As it turned out, Harry had a crush on a girl in his class, Dawn, who happened to live on the way to the disaster site. Rather than pedal our way back home, we spent the afternoon in Dawn's basement playing Monopoly.

She always had a couple of girlfriends at her house, which became the center of after-school activity for months. I mean innocent activity since we were only twelve and thirteen years old. At the time you either liked someone or you didn't. If a girl "liked" someone, that meant there was a serious romantic interest and the possibility of "going together." Dawn really liked Harry and Harry really liked Dawn.

Soon after one of Dawn's friends–I'll call her Maria–decided to "like" me. Maria relayed a message to me through Dawn, then Harry: she wanted to meet me at Dawn's house every day after school. While I was delighted that someone, anyone, liked me, I was also nervous and inexperienced. I'd never had a girlfriend and, even then, had little interest in getting one. I was thirteen and weighed eighty pounds.

Maria was one year behind me in grade school. She matured early, at least physically. She had long brown hair and dressed like a high school girl. Anyone who didn't know her and spotted her walking around the neighborhood, especially in warmer weather, might guess she was four or five years older than she was.

At the time she confessed to having had crushes on several other boys before me, including Eugene, a blond-haired Russian boy from 118th Street. I suspect Maria probably never met a cute boy she didn't like. Our relationship didn't last long. We got into arguments about silly things. When I played sports with my friends, she got mad because I didn't stop to fuss over her. Maria required a ton of attention. Because she was so attractive, she naturally drew a lot of it. She had a way of flirting with other boys that annoyed me. After all, we were sort of going steady, and I had cashed in some of my mother's extra Plaid Stamps at Plaid Land on Rockaway Boulevard and Liberty Avenue for a gold cross she'd hinted at.

One day she went to a girlfriend's house for an after-school party. When she got home she had hickeys on her neck. I'm talking fifth grade. Maria explained that Bridget had done it as a joke. It took me quite a while to figure out Bridget had not given Maria hickeys and that one of the boys at the party, I suspect Brian Campbell, probably did.

I had an honesty issue with that girl that I could never get past. One time we had an argument over something stupid, so I disappeared for a few days to teach her a lesson. She was upset and cried like a spoiled brat until I agreed to make up with her. Once she tracked me six blocks up to Liberty Avenue, where I had to run to get away from her. She left notes in my mailbox at home that I certainly didn't want my mother to read.

Other times she was calm and attentive. She gave me some of my earliest birds and bees education. One time she complained of cramps while I walked with her and her friend Cathy. I assumed she'd eaten a too-spicy slice at Tommy's Pizza. She referred to her condition as a visit from her cousin "Mabel." Cathy seemed to understand. I remained oblivious. The next day she handed me a booklet about menstruation and pregnancy. I was so naïve that the information was new to me. Live and learn.

Maria and her brother Ron were a little spoiled. They had the best clothes, music, and cars. Their mother raised the two of them pretty much on her own. Their father, who'd come from Italy, was strict. Since he didn't know his angelic daughter was going out with a boy, and an Irish one at that, the mother kept me a secret. She once told me in passing that her daughter was "boy crazy."

When Maria didn't get her way, she pouted. She once threw a temper tantrum on her mother because she wanted a friend to accompany her to the World's Fair in Flushing Meadows. Her older brother worked there scooping ice cream in one of the Belgian Village shops. Her mother, who worked at the same shop part-time, occasionally brought Maria along either for company or to keep an eye on her.

In any case, Maria's mother agreed I could come to the World's Fair for the day and keep Maria amused. The only stipulation was that Maria's annoying little brother had to tag along as we visited various exhibits. As hard as we tried, we could not shake the third wheel. We managed to get in a few hugs and kisses at the Futurama exhibit while the lights were down and the little brother stared into space.

Admission to the New York Worlds Fair, 1964, Flushing, Queens, New York.

Mostly, though, we were rarely alone together. We spent quite a bit of time pushing the limits of heavy petting in Carol Doyle's basement laundry room, but that was as far as it went. We were just kids. Besides, we were taught that anything beyond kissing was a sin.

Maria asked if she could see my bedroom one day. Maybe that idea came from me, actually. I had decorated the room with all kinds of teenage crap such as Beatles and Doors posters and high school banners. As it happened one summer afternoon, my mother and sister went to the Lefferts movie theater on Liberty Avenue to see a double feature. Maria and her friend Cathy, who was rather large and nicknamed the "Jolly Green Giant," rang my bell about an hour after my mother left the house.

I suggested that Cathy take my dog, Duchess, for a long walk so that Maria and I could take a "tour" of my room. As the tour was under way, the front door opened. In walked my mother and sister, followed by the Jolly Green Giant and my dog. Busted! I guess they only stayed for the first movie. *What do I do to minimize their suspicions about having a girl in my bedroom who dresses like a twenty-one-year-old divorcée? Hide her in the closet? But for how long? Ask her to jump out the window? She'd probably break a leg. Besides, what do I say about the dog walker?*

We both walked down the staircase together.

"Maria wanted to see my album collection and listen to some records," I said.

My mother kicked Maria out immediately.

"Back to your room!" she ordered me.

It took a few days for the excitement to wear down. Eventually, my face, which had been bright red from embarrassment, turned back to its normal dull red. The funny part of the whole escapade was that Maria and I *had* just been listening to records. But it certainly must have looked bad to my mother and sister.

My sister was more suspicious than my mother about what we could have been doing. I don't think my sister ever liked Maria. But that didn't stop her from including Maria in her bridal party when she later married my wonderful brother-in-law, Tony. My brother Danny's terrific wife, Diane, also was in that bridal party.

All wasn't bliss, however. My sister complained that Maria had embarrassed her at the beauty parlor the morning of the ceremony when she undertipped the hairdresser who combed out her hair. But Maria was so young. How could she know? It didn't help that the wedding gowns for the entire bridal party had been stolen from my brother-in-law's VW Beetle a week before the wedding. That put everyone on edge.

While attractive and with lots of curves here and there, Maria did possess a slightly larger than desirable nose. It never bothered me except when her mother insisted that she trim her bangs. That look made her nose more prominent. One afternoon while the gang and I played pool in Maria's finished basement, Tommy Manzo, one of the other boys, called her Pinocchio. His teasing annoyed me. When he said it one time too many times, I invited him outside for a brief fistfight. In no time he headed home to treat a very bloody nose. It was true irony–a nose for a nose.

While things weren't all bad, it was clear I wouldn't happily spend the rest of my life with Maria. We broke up when I was fourteen. Since I'd broken up with her numerous times, I expected that, as usual, we'd make up. But she spent the following Saturday frolicking at the airport with Cathy of dog walking fame and two boys from John Adams High School. Cathy couldn't wait to tell me about it. Maria never did.

That was it for me. Dating boys from John Adams was a deal breaker. I don't think she could ever get all the attention she required. She certainly didn't get it at home. It was lucky for me that we ended our tumultuous relationship after a year. The breakup opened the door for a life-altering experience.

Future Mrs. Herbert.

When I first signed up to deliver the *Long Island Press* shortly before my twelfth birthday, I was assigned a remote, crummy route of forty-five houses from 122nd Street to Lefferts Boulevard and 133rd Avenue. I had trouble making any money. Some customers forgot to pay their bills, which was deducted from my pay each week.

One customer called to complain because I'd gently tossed the newspaper to her rather than stop, get off my bike, and hand it to her. I guess I was always in a hurry. Another took a swing at me after I rang his bell around 6:30 on a Sunday morning in an aborted attempt to collect five weeks of past due bills. I never got that money, but they never got another *Long Island Press* newspaper.

One frigid Sunday morning with forty-five advertisement-crammed newspapers packed tightly in my front-loaded delivery basket, I rode off a low curb. My bike flipped over from back to front. What a crash. Papers flew out of the basket, up in the air, and on top of me. Complete sections blew down 111th Avenue in the wind. I quit the next day and got a job at Rexall Pharmacy on Rockaway Boulevard delivering drugs. Or should I say pharmaceuticals?

One summer day, as I rode my bike down Lefferts Boulevard, I noticed three really cute girls crossing the busy street. They were all my age. All had honey blonde hair and wore Army fatigue jackets and tight shorts. *Who is that one special girl?* I filed the sight away for future use.

CHAPTER SEVEN

BEACH BEER, FINES, AND SPANISH FLIES

1968-1970

As it happened, Billy Hawk, my best friend at the time, and I and a couple of other kids from Lefferts and Sutter (L&S) spent a summer afternoon at Rockaway Beach. We walked up to the 111th Street subway station on Liberty Avenue, which was one station further than the closest station, to catch the A train to Rockaway. We liked the 111th Street elevated station because it had no token clerk and we could crawl under the rotating gate and avoid paying the fifteen-cent token. Billy, Frankie, and I could just clear the bottom rail and slide under. Fat Ralph had to pay. He just wouldn't fit.

We liked going to the deli on 112th Street in Rockaway, too. It sold beer. We were only sixteen, two years younger than the legal drinking age. So we waited until an older guy came along. We offered to pay for a quart of his beer if he'd buy us some Colt 45 Malt Liquor. The plan never failed.

Photo by Paula Borowska on Unsplash

We hid under the boardwalk at Rockaway Beach and drank our quarts of Colt 45 out of a paper bag. Why be obvious? I must have wandered outside the safe zone one particular day. Two cops on the boardwalk spotted me from above. They signaled for me to come up the stairs. Like an idiot, I did. I should have run back under the boardwalk and disappeared.

"I see you're drinking beer," one cop said. "You have an ID?"

I produced my student ID from Bishop Loughlin Memorial, the highly rated Brooklyn-based diocesan high school.

"This is your lucky day," he said. "I went to Loughlin. Besides, I just wrote my last summons a few minutes ago."

"Thank you, Officer," I said, turning to resume happy hour under the boardwalk.

The other cop stopped me.

"I have plenty of tickets left in my book," he said, "and I'd be happy to write one in your honor."

He did. That ticket required me to appear in person at the Long Island City County of Queens Courthouse some thirty days later. This was a problem for a couple of reasons. First, I didn't want my mother to know I was drinking beer at the beach. Second, my appearance was set for 10 a.m. on a September school day. A special and risky plan was needed.

I talked my girlfriend into disguising her voice, pretending to be my mother, and calling the Bishop Loughlin attendance office. She informed them that "little Tommy" was sick and could not possibly make it to school that day. Miraculously, the ploy worked.

Instead of going to school, I went to court. I was alone and must have looked like I was twelve years old. The judge looked at the summons, looked down at me, and took mercy. He sentenced me to a five-dollar fine. I'd brought fifteen dollars, just to be safe, paid in cash, and headed back to South Ozone Park, feeling like I'd beaten the system. My mother never found out. Success!

The following summer Billy Hawk and I were back at Rockaway drinking beer under the boardwalk. A cop spotted Billy and issued him a summons for underage drinking. I told Billy not to sweat it. I told him about my five-dollar fine. Confident he'd face the same fate, we both went to court in Long Island City to take care of the summons three or four weeks after the ticket was issued.

Alarmingly, Billy's judge was not amused. He fined Billy fifty dollars! Neither of us had that kind of money. Billy was given ten days to return and pay the fine. Another special and risky plan was needed.

We decided to host a card game behind the VFW and provide free Harvey Wallbangers and beer to anyone who played. The games ranged from blackjack to Indian poker. We charged five dollars a head for a seat at the table and had a number of guests throughout the evening. We didn't quite make fifty dollars but we easily made enough to cover the drink costs.

Billy was an excellent player, especially against less sophisticated players we called suckers. He had an artistic ability to shave the edges of certain cards to help him guess what they might be. An occasional extra black mark on the back of picture cards also came in handy.

We needed another fund-raiser to raise the balance of the fifty-buck fine. A plan was hatched for Fat Ralph to purchase an ounce of pot from one of the kids at the Conduit Park near the Belt Parkway. The pot was supplemented with oregano and divided it into five-dollar ("nickel") bags. It was sort of like the loaves and the fishes. You could make more bags if you added the oregano. The nickel bags sold in one weekend to the nerds who hung out at 115th Street and Rockaway Boulevard. The gang sold enough to cover the cost of Billy's fine and make a small profit. There may even have been a little pot left over for the gang to enjoy the following weekend. Ingenious!

The cops sure taught us a lesson. We funded the beer fine with the proceeds from a marijuana yard sale. I don't remember anyone in my group ever doing anything like that again. One and done.

Thomas Downs, who was in my class at Our Lady of Perpetual Help, also attended Bishop Loughlin from 1966 to 1970. I knew him, but we weren't close. Thomas, not one of the better-looking guys in the neighborhood, was naïve as to affairs of the ladies. He and his band of buddies from 111th Street and Rockaway Boulevard near Aqueduct Racetrack were behind most of us when it came to alcohol, pot, and girl chasing.

In a moment of magical inspiration, we decided to add "Spanish Flies" to our offerings. The word on the street was that "Spanish Flies" would turn your average South Queens schoolgirl into an insatiable nymph who'd do anything with anyone at any time.

We had no idea what a "Spanish Fly" looked like. Neither did Thomas Downs. We skimmed a handful of dead flies off a neighbor's above-ground swimming pool and put three or four of them in a plastic bag. We sold them to Thomas Downs for five dollars a bag. It wasn't right, but it sure was funny. I often wondered if Thomas ever actually got one of the girls to swallow those flies.

A few months later, a strange thing happened to me as I drove my 1960 Chevy Impala home from my girlfriend's house on Lefferts Boulevard. I had a friend in the car. We headed west on Sutter Avenue around 116th Street. The car was a $100 special with what I called "strong arm power steering" and "anti-stop brakes," the opposite of anti-lock brakes. I had bald snow tires on the front and rear. The master cylinder was leaking and I had to pump the brakes a few times to stop. The car reeked of brake fluid.

Suddenly and out of nowhere, an unmarked police car pulled me over and four plainclothes cops surrounded my car. They pulled both of us out, searched us, and asked us to empty our pockets on the hood. While two cops questioned me, the other two thoroughly searched my car. They even emptied the ashtray on the trunk, looking for a roach, the very end tip of a joint.

"What are you looking for?" I asked.

The answer was simple.

"Drugs," one of them said.

They were convinced we had drugs.

"What's that awful smell?" another officer demanded to know.

"Brake fluid," I said.

He asked again. He didn't believe me until I showed him the leaking master cylinder. Somewhat annoyed and disappointed, they sent us on our way. That night there were no drugs on us or in the car. Lucky thing!

I wonder to this day who tipped off those cops. Could it have been one of the nerds from 115th Street? Perhaps it was Thomas Downs, who may have discovered that all "Spanish Flies" do is make girls throw up.

CHAPTER 8

THE FREE CASE OF BEER

1966-1970

The way to prove you were eighteen, the legal drinking age in New York City in the 1960s, was to show your draft card. Naturally, many of us had fake ones by the time we were sixteen. Before that we bribed an older guy or someone with a fake card to purchase a couple of quarts of Colt 45 or a pint of cheap vodka. Then we made the screwdrivers or Harvey Wallbangers needed to get our weekend off to a flying start.

My fake draft card had an error in one description field. I had typed "Broun" instead of "Brown" in the hair color section. I had also added a distinguishing facial characteristic–"Cleft in Chin." Everyone looked at my chin. No one caught the misspelling.

The goal was to get drunk as quickly and inexpensively as possible but still be able to walk and talk straight by the time we got home–just in case our parents actually spoke to us.

Occasionally, one of the gang borrowed booze from their parents' liquor cabinet and donated it to the weekend festivities. On one occasion Billy Hawk or Mooch poured whiskey into pill vials intended for other purposes. The vials were easy to smuggle in and out of the house. To replace the displaced liquor they added tap water to the whiskey bottles, which suspicious but naïve parents had so cleverly level marked.

Billy and Mooch couldn't dilute the whiskey too often, though. Sooner or later someone would sit down for a stiff scotch on the rocks and discover they were drinking tap water on the rocks with a splash of Dewar's. When it finally happened and despite passionate denials, we lost one of the gang for at least a week.

Photo by Mateo Abrahan on Unsplash

We hit pay dirt one Saturday afternoon when a beer delivery truck pulled up in front of the deli on Lefferts and Sutter (L&S). I jokingly asked the driver if he had any left-over beer. He laughed.

"It's my last stop for the day," he said. "The truck is empty except for some deposit returns on the top rack. If you can find any beer up there, you can have it."

Up I went. Sure enough, there was one lonely case of Pabst Blue Ribbon. We quickly commandeered it and carried it to the back of the VFW parking lot for happy hour later. I'm not sure what eventually caused me to throw up that night–the warm beer or the pickles from Numson's Deli.

Some Saturday mornings Billy Hawk and I traveled to Our Lady of Mercy parish in Brownsville, Brooklyn, where my brother was the assigned priest. We took a bus and two subway connections and then briskly walked from the station to the church. The neighborhood was rough so we moved as quickly as possible. Once there we taught CCD to students who attended the local public school.

On our way home one day we saw a gum-dispensing machine bolted to a steel column at the Eastern Parkway station. It had a coin slot with a turning mechanism that allowed little boxes of Chicklets to drop to the bottom slot. We turned the crank one time without depositing the nickel or dime required and got a box of gum for free. We turned it again and again. Out came more boxes of Chicklets. We were having such a good time emptying the gum machine, we let two trains pass. By the time the next one arrived, we had at least one hundred little boxes. We stuffed them in our pants and shirts. For weeks we had the freshest breath in South Ozone Park.

Frankie D, another of my best friends, had a calm, steady demeanor but he was always up for an adventure. At times he was shy, though, and always reserved in the company of girls. The very mention of talking to neighborhood coeds turned his cheeks red.

Billy, Frankie, and I drank our first beers together, smoked our first joints, and chased a lot of girls. Frankie's parents were strict. His father was a night watchman and his mother worked weekends at the telephone company in Jamaica.

But one night Frankie got permission to have a sleep-over. Our plan was simple. At 4 p.m. Billy and I would meet Joey Cogiano, who was eighteen, at the deli and pay him to purchase six quarts of Colt 45 Malt Liquor. We would buy hero sandwiches, chips, and pickles. Then we would walk down to Frankie's house, stash all the goods in his yard, and wait for his mom to leave for work. We planned to drink our beer at Frankie's and later crash a little party on Sutter and 118th Street. We were definitely not invited to the party, where we expected to meet some guys we didn't like.

We had just opened our first bottles of malt liquor, which always tasted better when consumed from a paper bag with a straw, when Frankie's mother returned. In her haste to get to work she'd forgotten something. She pushed open the door to Frankie's bedroom, stepped over Billy, who was sprawled on the floor, and narrowly missed kicking over a bottle of Colt 45. She reached over me and grabbed something, possibly a sweater, from the closet, and vanished. We were stunned. She was so focused on getting her stuff that she missed seeing or smelling six quarts of malt liquor. Close call but we got away with it.

Later that night Billy, Frankie, and I joined up with a few other guys who hung out at the candy store on Lefferts Boulevard and Sutter Avenue. We all headed for the party. By then we were probably a few gin and tonics or Harvey Wallbangers on top of the Colt 45. We rushed into the dark alley next to the house where the party was taking place. Fifteen yards from the back-door entrance to the party, someone came out of nowhere and either kicked or sucker punched me. I was down for the count.

As the brawl escalated, everyone scattered. I got up and continued down the alley to the back fence that separated the property from the one behind it. As I jumped the low chain-link fence, the owner took a swing at me as I ran by him. A swing and a miss! Clearly, it was my day to get attacked.

I thought, *I better get out of here before someone calls the cops.* What happened next is a blur. I lost track of Billy, Frankie, and the rest of the gang. I couldn't show up at home because I was supposed to sleep at Frankie's house that night. I was in no shape to go home, anyway. I curled up in a storefront next to the VFW. As the night went on, the air got colder. I was more and more uncomfortable.

Eventually, bruised and battered, I walked down to Frankie's house and tapped on the first-floor window of his bedroom. I woke him up, but he let me in and gave me ice for the lump on my head. I woke up the next day with a huge headache. Because of the fight or the beer? We were bad kids back then and only sixteen years old to boot.

CHAPTER 9

TRIPS AND THE FRESH AIR FUND

1966-1970

When I was eight or nine, I was perfectly content to play in the streets with my friends all summer. I wore the same pair of dungarees for weeks at a time without laundering. It was heaven. But someone thought it'd be a good idea to expose me to serene country living.

In early July my mother told me I was going away for a Fresh Air Fund vacation the following Saturday. She called it "a two-week escape where you'll ride horses, milk cows, and help out around the farm with other kids your age." I wasn't thrilled about being shipped off to places unknown, but I was excited to hang out with horses.

When that Saturday morning arrived, a parish priest drove me to Grand Central Station in Manhattan. He put a ribbon with a name tag and a destination address around my neck and handed me off to a grumpy conductor. I was escorted to a seat on a train headed north to Brewster, a suburb. I was nine and alone. I'd never been on a train like that before.

When I hopped off in Brewster, the family I was supposed to meet wasn't there. Eventually they arrived and drove me to their farm. Actually, it wasn't a farm. It was more like the New Rochelle house where Dick Van Dyke and Mary Tyler Moore lived on TV. It had a yard, some trees, and a cat. But no cows, no goats, no sheep. And no damn horses. They didn't even have a pony or a mule. I felt tricked and disappointed.

The Apollo family had a mom (Jewish), a dad (Italian and a drinker), and two daughters, ages eight and ten. For the first two or three days, I was a novelty. After that I was treated like a pest. During the second week the parents openly argued. I was severely homesick. I will say, though, that the Apollo family made an effort to celebrate my birthday. They gave me a cupcake with a candle and a plastic ninety-nine-cent covered wagon with four plastic horses from the local five and dime. Finally, horses! I was glad to get out when my sentence was up.

Several years later, after we moved to Queens, my brother Vic offered to take me and two of my friends on a canoe trip on Long Lake in Upstate New York. It was 1966. I was fourteen. We paddled from Long Lake up the Racquet River to Tupper Lake. It was great to camp out, tell ghost stories, and enjoy the serenity of the river and lakes. We roughed it for three days.

After paddling such a long distance, we all had blisters. At times the currents became too dangerous to follow in the canoes, so we carried them–a portage that lasted for whole sections of the river. For me, this was like the Boy Scouts. I wasn't allowed to join the real Boy Scouts because the local troop was based in a Protestant Church, not a Catholic one.

Billy Hawk and Regis Manzo bonded on that trip. We had such a good time that we asked Vic to take us again. Vic was always willing to do interesting things during the summer months. Everyone heard what a great time we'd had the first year and wanted to go. He agreed to take five of my Queens friends the following year.

The fact we were with a Catholic priest put parents at ease. Little did parents know, Victor was on the liberal side when it came to disciplining the canoe gang. In year two we were fifteen or sixteen and eager to assert our independence. By that time most of us had been experimenting with alcohol, girls, and weed. But the second canoe trip got off to a bad start for Billy Hawk, Frankie Sans, Frank Duban, Vic, Fat Ralph, and me. We stopped at an upstate restaurant for breakfast before renting the canoes and equipment.

Victor Herbert, Canoe Trip Guide, 1967, Tupper Lake, New York.

We had packed for every eventuality, including suntan lotion, bug spray, gloves to avoid the blisters we'd gotten the year before, and several bottles of the cheapest vodka, gin, and whiskey our fake draft cards could buy. As we excitedly discussed the days ahead, someone realized we'd forgotten to pack salt and pepper.

In the mind of Billy Hawk, it was never a matter of bad conscience to clip anything needed or desired.

"Don't worry," he told us. "I have it covered."

Generally, Billy had character and integrity, but there were noticeable gaps in their consistency when it came to acquiring things.

We'd arrived at the sleepy Long Lake restaurant early in the morning and were among its only customers. As we left, the waitress noticed the salt and pepper shakers had disappeared.

"If they do not reappear immediately," she threatened, "I'll have you all arrested."

Miraculously, Billy located the missing condiments in his left front pocket. The day was saved.

The first night we camped in a clearing infested with mini frogs. They weren't there when we pitched the tents along the river. When it got dark, though, they arrived in large numbers. The noise was deafening. We sang Beatles songs. Vic told scary stories. He had Frankie Sans and Ralphie so nervous, neither could sleep. Both refused to turn off their flashlights. What caught Ralphie's imagination the most was the one about the crazed scoutmaster who'd lost his mind near Long Lake and chopped up campers with an ax.

Ralphie was a large and funny human being but certainly not a seasoned camper or outdoorsman. On the first night he insisted on using the duffel bag that contained most of our food as a pillow. Vic warned him bears and other animals could smell the food a mile away. He asked Ralphie to hang the duffel so high in a tree that the animals couldn't get at it.

When we woke the next morning, it was apparent critters had gnawed through the canvas bag during the night. The bag, which had been half eaten, had gaping holes in it. Animals must have been crawling all over Ralphie while he slept.

The trip was uneventful until early the second day when Ralphie flipped the canoe he and Frankie Sans were piloting. Unfortunately, as the canoe flipped, the damaged duffel bag containing the remainder of our food slipped into the river and sank. It should have been tethered to the canoe, but it hadn't been.

What do you do when you're more than a day's travel time from civilization in either direction with six hungry guys and three bottles of cheap booze? We did the only thing we could: we broke into a ranger's cabin. We had waited for the ranger to return. When he didn't, we went in through a window and relieved him of some peanut butter and crackers. We were nice enough to leave a note explaining our plight before running back to the canoes, jumping in, and paddling as fast as we could.

Later that afternoon we found a campsite close to a bridge where a road passed overhead. Billy Hawk and I volunteered to paddle there, a couple of miles upstream. We hitched a ride to the nearest town, found a food store, bought supplies and food, hitchhiked back to the river, and paddled back to the campsite. We were welcomed liked heroes for providing a decent meal of Dinty Moore stew and warm booze.

We stowed the food in a tree overnight. What was left rode with me and Vic in the lead canoe the following day.

We were growing up and some guys were headed in the wrong direction. Not too many years later, Fat Ralph died of a heroin overdose. It seemed to me that the guys who went to the Catholic high schools such as Bishop Loughlin and Cathedral High School avoided the worst temptations of the neighborhood. In the meantime, some of the John Adams gang who already made bad decisions took them to another level.

CHAPTER 10

THE FIGHTS

1962-1972

We had plenty of wise guys in Queens. I don't mean mobsters though we had plenty of those, too, but a wide assortment of kids who could annoy each other. It seemed like each block had a million kids. Typically, there were thirty individual houses per block. Being good Catholics, many families had an average of four to six kids.

On one particular block–122nd Street between Sutter Avenue and 133rd Avenue–I counted a dozen boys between age twelve and sixteen. The same was true on Sutter Avenue and 118th Street.

The corner of Lefferts Boulevard and Sutter Avenue, considered the center of activities, attracted forty or fifty kids coming and going, especially in summer. Since we were too young to drive, this corner served us well. It was easily within walking distance for many.

Over the years I witnessed a dozen fights there. An argument could break out over a disputed call in boxball. Games of coin toss also got nasty: the guy who got the coin closest to the wall got to keep the other guy's money. There were lots of card games going on all the time, too-poker, blackjack, and Acey-Deucey for money. Cheating was rare but not unheard of. Once, I saw Steve, one of the 122nd Street kids, and an honest guy, bet the pot two times in a row and lose twice with unbeatable hands. It cost him ten bucks.

I got into a fight with one kid, Paul, who scored a direct hit on my nose with a peashooter. He laughed. I went after him. He ducked and rolled, taking my legs out from under me, which made me fall on my elbows. Both were scraped raw on the asphalt. We wrestled until somebody broke it up. It was a friendly fight, which I would have scored 10–9 in favor of Paul.

The next morning I rang his bell and called him out to complete the battle. That one was more punching than wrestling, which was better for me. It ended in a headlock on the ground with me on top. My honor and reputation had been restored. Score that one 10–8 in my favor.

Paul was a nice-looking guy who attracted girls in the neighborhood, including one I dated briefly. Later he and I became good friends. He tutored me in Algebra the day before my final exam, which was enough to help me score a 75 percent and avoid summer school.

He liked to fight, though. I saw him throw sand in a kid's face on 122nd Street, which temporarily blinded the kid. That was settled the next day when Paul took a beating.

Another kid on Sutter Avenue paid a little too much attention to one of the girls I liked. He was well dressed, had money, and lived in one of the nicest homes in the neighborhood. Though big, he wasn't known to fight. One day on a dare I walked up to him and punched him in the face.

"You're a nut!" he yelled before going home to get his mother. I don't think he forgave me for that. I don't blame him.

As our gang got older, fights got more serious. One night Mooch was standing in front of the candy store on

Lefferts and Sutter (L&S), minding his business, when a group of thugs from another area came looking for trouble. Not one to back down, Mooch, who was with a few buddies but nevertheless outnumbered, lost several teeth when he got smacked in the mouth with a pipe. Another time Bill had his head smashed into the rear bumper of a parked car, causing a bloody mess.

I wasn't present at either event. Had I been, I believe we could have talked our way out of the situations.

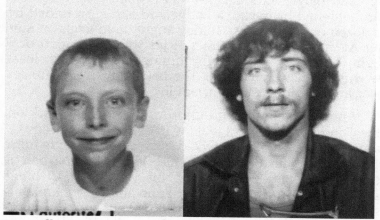

You talking to me? 1966 (left) and 1970.

A park up near the Belt Parkway Conduit had its own crowd. Two of the local punks beat up Bill's younger brother, Michael, at the handball courts one night. He came home bruised and battered. Bill called for me, Al, and Mooch. Off we went on our bikes, looking for revenge. It turned out to be a triple event. Bill caught the two brothers who jumped Michael and took them on, one at a time, with an assist from Mooch. Al battled another while I bumped into one of the dumbest John Adams dropouts: the guy had caused me trouble involving a girl and a trip to Kennedy Airport that I'd never forgotten about.

"Shrimp!" he said when he caught sight of me.

While I only weighed about 130 pounds, I'd been beaten up enough that I'd learned how to fight pretty well. He landed the first one. I landed the next ten.

On another occasion a fairly large group of teens from 115th Street and Rockaway Boulevard descended on our corner looking for Regis. While not a very popular guy, Regis had somehow managed to catch the attention of the former boyfriend of Linda, a cute little blonde. Let's call the guy Guido. He had a best friend built like a pro football player although he was probably only sixteen. Emboldened by having a bodyguard and surrounded by a dozen of his flunkies, Guido caught up to Regis on Sutter Avenue and 118th Street. Regis wanted no part of a fight, but Guido insisted by hitting Regis with at least twenty unanswered hooks. The best Regis could muster was an occasional, "Quit it, Guido!" Fight over.

Another really bad group from up near the park on the Conduit was always looking to fight. One was Tony C., a notorious dirty fighter who'd once stabbed a guy from 115th Street with a large metal file. He kept it in his belt in case a fair fight wasn't going his way. Tony C. hung around with a group of future heroin addicts, including a guy we'll call Ronnie, who looked like an extra from one of the *West Side Story* gangs. He walked with a pronounced bop and usually wore a muscle tee shirt to show off his muscular 5'3" body. Usually, he was accompanied by Eddie Woo from the laundromat, Wayne the stutterer, and little Will the car thief.

As I walked back from Numson's German Deli next to the candy store, I heard a ruckus. Ronnie was whipping one of the older guys from the neighborhood with an antenna he'd torn off a parked car. Meanwhile, Tony C. was swinging his belt buckle at the same guy's girlfriend, who was trying to break up the fight. In an effort to help her, I jumped in the middle to make peace. I knew both sides of the battle. Besides, my big, strong best friend John was with me. Within seconds, the police arrived and the fight ended. It was a good thing, too, because John had left me there and run home to the safety of his mother's basement. Nice guy but no balls!

Billy Hawk and I once went shopping at the Green Acres Mall in Valley Stream to pick up a few things. We occasionally lifted merchandise without dealing with the inconvenience of standing on line and paying. Billy could power shop like a man possessed. He once went into the fitting room at Macy's and emerged wearing three different pairs of pants. He looked fat. He was fearless. Though good with pants, sweaters were his specialty. Need a Christmas gift for mom? No problem. Billy stole anything and everything on demand.

On the walk back to our car that day, a fight erupted out of thin air. This often happened when Billy was around. He was whipping some guy with the buckle end of his leather belt. I was tangled up with a different guy who wasn't cooperating with my efforts to put him on the ground. I decided to pull his sweatshirt over his head so I could more easily punch him without running the risk of getting punched. The fight was over in thirty seconds. Why it started in the first place, I couldn't say. Neither could the other guys. Before we left they asked us, "Was that a fraternity prank?"

The Steak and Brew bar brawl the night before my eighteenth birthday was one of the worst fights. The brew, not the steak, attracted us to the Manhattan restaurant. Customers could drink as much beer as they liked during dinner at no additional charge. Since we all had bogus draft cards, being underage wasn't a problem. The tricky part was finding a waitress to bring the pitchers. They all seemed to hide.

On that particular night, there were four or five of us, including Billy Hawk and a few high school buddies. One of the guys, who had a black belt in karate, got aggressive when moderately intoxicated. We met a great group of guys from Staten Island, though. Everybody was having fun until five or six lifeguards from Glen Cove, Long Island arrived and sparks flew. Chairs and punches were thrown. Beer mugs were smashed. The restaurant turned into a saloon out of a Western movie.

The restaurant manager chased me around the dining room during the melee. I escaped him in the revolving door at the main entrance. I couldn't leave my friends in the middle of a fight, though, so I revolved back into the restaurant and brawl.

"I have called the police!" the manager yelled. We put money on our table to cover our dinners and abruptly left. As we walked out the front door, we heard approaching sirens. We hid in bushes across the street as three or four police cars descended on the restaurant. It had been a blast and none of us got hurt, which was a miracle.

Turned out, Steve, a great guy with movie star looks and a hot temper, hadn't liked the way one of the Glen Cove lifeguards looked at him. He mentioned it to Billy. They decided between themselves to each randomly pick one lifeguard and punch them. Unfortunately, they both chose the same guy. It would have been helpful if they'd clued me in.

I stupidly returned to the same restaurant the following night to celebrate my birthday with my family. With thousands of restaurants in New York City, why did I return to this one the night after we tore it up? I must have thought the manager wouldn't recognize me or perhaps that he'd have the night off. The minute I walked in, he was on me. He was incredulous that I'd have the nerve to come back.

"Leave! Leave!" he yelled. "I will not serve you!"

I pulled him aside.

"Look, I'm the guy you chased around the restaurant, but I was trying to break up the fight, not participate in it," I said.

Surprisingly, he bought it and seated us. On our way out he politely asked me how dinner was.

Another time Steve, Billy, and I were invited on a Fordham University ski trip. At the time Bill and I worked at the phone company with two Fordham students. As the drinking increased, so did the lunacy. Steve and Billy joined Fordham students in the hotel lobby as they watched a televised Fordham–Marquette basketball game. Just to be difficult, our two guys cheered every time Marquette scored a basket. A Fordham kid kicked a plastic ice bucket across the room, accidentally hitting Steve and bloodying his lip. Steve hit the guy.

Just as the mini brawl started, I entered the lobby and saw Steve holding another Fordham guy by the shirt collar. He was about to flatten him. Meanwhile, a third Fordham guy raised a beer bottle to hit Steve over the head. Steve didn't see it coming. I delivered a hard overhand right and caught the guy flush. He went down hard. When one of the Fordham guys was taken to a hospital, the three of us left earlier than we'd planned. We never looked back. None of us could afford police involvement.

Sometimes after playing softball we went to a rough bar on Atlantic Avenue and Lefferts Boulevard. One night, in walked Mooch's brother-in-law, Luke, who argued over a pool game with a guy I'd never seen before. I interceded on Luke's behalf. Before I knew it, I was on the sidewalk facing an opponent who appeared much larger outside than he had in the bar. Once again, my mouth had been faster than my brain or my fists.

I was committed, though, so I threw the first punch, which missed and sailed over my elusive opponent's head. I spun off-balance. Next thing I knew, the guy was on my back, choking me from behind. I attempted to flip him over my shoulder, a maneuver I'd seen in many movies. He resisted, spun me around, and delivered a flurry of punches, few of which missed. I got a few more shots off but to no avail. I was getting clobbered.

Fortunately, somebody broke it up. I was black and blue the next morning. The next time I saw Luke, I had a question.

"I thought you might jump in to help me," I said.

"Yeah," he replied, "and I thought you could fight!"

That was my last bar fight.

Chapter 11

THE CARS

1969-1974

I n the late sixties and early seventies, we got our driving
licenses at the age of seventeen, provided we attended
and passed a certified drivers education class. Still high
school students, we didn't have a lot of money to invest in
a quality used car. We suffered from serious cases of "lack
of funds."

New cars were totally out of the question though a
spanking brand-new Plymouth Duster went for $1,999.99
plus tax. For us, that was a lot. Most of us came from
working-class families. Our moms were housewives. Our
dads struggled just to pay the rent or mortgage. There
wasn't a lot of discretionary cash to buy junior a car–or
the car insurance that came along with it. At least gas was
relatively cheap at thirty to thirty-five cents a gallon. If you
bought a full tank, you might even get a Flintstones glass.

Our best option was the really low end of the used car
market–the bottom of the barrel where only the desper-
ate shopped. There was also the *Buy Lines* and classified
sections of the *Long Island Press* or *Daily News* or *Post*.

Occasionally, through word of mouth, a miracle occurred and a car became available for a hundred dollars
or less. These were destined for the junkyard, of course.

Most of these cars were best suited for hospice, not the streets of Queens.

My first car was a huge 1960 Dodge Phoenix donated to me by a Catholic priest who was a friend of my brother Vic. This beast was only getting around 8 mpg and was killing me. I typically pulled into a gas station and asked for a dollar's worth of regular. A fill-up was a fantasy, which is why I never got a free Flintstones glass.

While I will always be eternally grateful for my first rolling motel on wheels, there were issues. The car overheated at any temperature above 80 degrees. The rear bumper was damaged, its right side sticking straight up and out like the tusk of a deranged rhinoceros. The AM radio had static on all five channels, and the driver's side mirror dangled by a wire. It was rusting badly around the gas tank, too, and was missing a hubcap.

I drove my friends to the beach, but they got tired of pulling over on the way. I had to let the radiator cool off and then add more water without cracking the block. Sick of getting picked on about the rear bumper, I remedied the situation the old-fashioned way–without the services of a qualified collision shop. We found a warehouse with a concrete loading dock and repeatedly rammed the car, driving fast and backwards, until the rear bumper aligned itself. It never occurred to us that this technique wasn't good for the health and welfare of the rest of the car.

A few days later the Phoenix started bucking when operating in DRIVE. We moved the gear selector to LOW, which solved the problem for about a week. The ramming had damaged the push-button transmission system. Eventually, we were down to REVERSE. We drove the car backwards around the neighborhood. When that went, we junked it for twenty-five dollars.

My second car was a Rambler with more rust and rot than the Titanic after the iceberg hit it. That seventy-five-dollar beauty collapsed on Rockaway Boulevard and narrowly missed crashing into the front gate of the Aqueduct

Racetrack. Both front wheels pancaked simultaneously, requiring a well-controlled crash landing. It would have cost more to tow it than I paid for it. So I junked it at the salvage yard across from Americana Lanes near the subway El on Liberty Avenue.

Next came a 1960 Chevy Impala featuring anti-stop brakes and a leaky carburetor. When I stopped I had to pump the brakes because of a questionable master cylinder issue. I purchased that piece of junk for one hundred dollars from the father of a good friend who had driven it to work. He was a fireman in the Brownsville section of Brooklyn. The car had well over a hundred thousand miles on it–and looked it. Like the others, it had no seat belts, airbags, AC, or any other fancy equipment.

When the power steering broke, I drove without it. Always safety conscious, I added a pair of nearly bald studded snow tires. I don't exactly recall why I put them on the front instead of the back. Without the power steering, it was tricky to steer, anyway, without a great deal of extra effort. The Impala was my ride to high school in the Bedford Stuyvesant section of Brooklyn. Once my friend Sal and I replaced the carburetor on the way to school on Atlantic Avenue in Brooklyn. I had to carry a rebuilt spare carburetor because they leaked so often. I dumped that car a year after I got it when I was rear-ended at a red light: the transmission slipped and eventually failed.

The cars were endless, and they were all bad. There was a 1968 Chevy Belvedere I bought for five hundred dollars in the winter. It wasn't until the summer that I discovered the AC didn't work.

There was a VW Beetle with no gas gauge. How about the Buick Skylark convertible that had an electrical short and a mind of its own? Or the Datsun 1200 that overheated and blew up on the Walt Whitman Bridge in Philadelphia on a hot, sticky July day? That car remained in Philadelphia.

Carrmela in Montreal in the winter of 1972 with the Datsun Model 1200.

I acquired a used 1966 fire engine red Mustang from a friend. It was hot! No, I mean it was really hot since the AC didn't work. That one cost me fifteen hundred dollars. Its two recurring problems drove me nuts. The brake calipers had been bathed in motor oil, or something, in the past, and the rotors were out of round. Since the car had a four-speed manual transmission, I had to shift frequently. Unfortunately, the reverse gear had to be pulled up on a pin that was connected to a cable that put the car in reverse. That cable and linkage broke at least once a month. On a date at the Sunrise Drive-In one night, I had to borrow a hoop earring from my girlfriend, crawl under the car, and use the earring to reconnect the linkage. Somehow we made it home.

There's an old saying, If it ain't broke, don't fix it. This didn't sink in for me and my gang. We were always monkeying with our jalopies. It was never enough for the cars to look good. They had to sound good, too. At the time Thrush Mufflers, a popular accessory, were on sale at Times Square Stores. These aftermarket, expensive mufflers rivaled the Glasspack exhaust system and made a car sound like a race car on steroids. I had to have one.

It was agreed that Anthony Sosso, a well-known street mechanic and Bishop Loughlin classmate, would do the installation. He had a part-time job at a supermarket during the day and could only install the Thrush system around 7 p.m. He was confident he could get it done within an hour and comfortable doing the work on the street in front of my house on 107th Street. We didn't have access to a garage.

We pulled the right side of the car up on the curb to gain access space underneath. We jacked up the right rear end to the max. Naturally, the existing mufflers were bolted tightly, and the rusty hardware was difficult to remove. It was getting darker by the minute. Our flashlights strained to provide enough illumination to see the entire procedure clearly.

What was supposed to take one hour took three. This installation cut into our scheduled drinking time at Al's Stereo Bar on Jamaica Avenue. Finally, Anthony scraped his last knuckle and tightened the final nut on the U-Bolt. The car was lowered off the jack and onto the street.

I was thrilled with my new Thrush mufflers and the growling sound when I revved the 289-cubic-inch engine. I was probably happier than my 107th Street neighbors, who heard me coming and going from a mile away.

The next day on the way to school, I approached a very busy intersection on Flatbush Avenue as the light was red. Several cars ahead had already stopped. As I applied the brakes, the pedal went straight to the floor without warning. I turned to my friend Pete and said, "We have no brakes!"

When Anthony installed the mufflers the night before, he had failed to relocate and fasten the dangling brake lines safely out of contact with the mufflers. As the mufflers got hot, one of them melted the rubber section of the brake line. Out came the brake fluid, so vitally important to activating the brakes. Just as we were about to hit the car in front of us at the light, an opening appeared in the adjacent lane, designed for traffic flowing in the opposite direction. Desperately searching for the emergency brake, I pulled left into that lane just as the light changed. Amazingly, we were lucky to slide through the intersection, avoiding traffic from both directions, and head for the curb on the opposite side of the street. There we ground to a halt before catastrophe struck.

Shaken and alert, we made it to school and put the car up for sale a week later. Got twelve hundred dollars for it. Probably should have kept it. A 1966 Mustang fastback is probably worth fifteen thousand dollars today. Who knew?

CHAPTER 12

THE STREAKER AND THE MUFFS

1969-1974

The tan brick building at 140 West Street in Lower Manhattan is especially significant to me. For five years I worked and played there with New York Telephone's best repair service technicians. My best friend at the time, Billy Hawk, and I were hired as part-timers in 1969, during our final year of high school. I milked that assignment until 1974 when I graduated CUNY's Brooklyn College.

Our work schedules varied based on school hours. Typically, though, we signed in at around 4 p.m. and worked until 10 p.m. during the school year. Earlier in the year, during the summer, we worked additional hours. The arrangement was good because 90 percent of the regular staff, including most managers, left at 5 p.m.

Billy worked there only a couple of years. He left in 1971 in the midst of a labor strike. Even as part-timers we were required to join the union, Communication Workers of America, and pay dues. We honored the picket lines and found ourselves out of work for seven months. Billy started driving trucks and dropped out of college. I traveled to Europe with my brother Victor and his wife, Minnie. I collected twenty-seven dollars per week in unemployment insurance with no help at all from the union.

My initial job at the Repair Service Bureau was "Searcher." I located records for business and residential customers who had called us reporting trouble with their phone service. As a Searcher, I was free to roam the Repair Service Bureau looking for paper-based telephone equipment records that were manually moved from one station to the next. The job fit naturally into a seamless system.

When a customer called to report a problem, a Repair Service Attendant created a trouble ticket, pulled the permanent customer record from a bin, and forwarded both to the Testers, who were mostly great guys. They diagnosed the problem and dispatched a Repair Technician or Frame Mechanic to address the issue. Testing was a monotonous job, though. Testers stayed at their consoles all day, taking fifteen-minute breaks in the morning and afternoon. For lunch they got forty-five-minutes. While searching for records I developed strong personal relationships with many testers and their managers. They seemed genuinely interested in my life as a college student, and their job piqued my curiosity as a possible post-college career path.

One of the best things about working for the phone company was their softball team. New York Telephone sponsored a league that played on Randall's Island near the Triborough Bridge. Our team was appropriately named the Muffs. We didn't win many games but always had a lot of fun.

The company provided each team with fifty dollars per game for sandwiches and beer. Naturally, we used the money for beer. Since our office was at the southern tip of Manhattan and the fields were at the northern tip, and traffic was terrible, team members were allowed to leave work an hour early. Beer drinking began immediately.

The day following the games, results and stats were posted in the breakroom along with the "Hole in the Glove" award for the player who made the most errors. I'm sure I won my share of those.

About the only way to get fired from New York Telephone was by being chronically late or absent. If you were late sometimes, you went through a multi-step disciplinary program. If you were late enough times, they forced you out and the union couldn't save you. Goofing off, drinking during lunch, and being rude to customers was fine. But not being late.

Billy Hawk and I occasionally signed the attendance book for each other to avoid any lateness or absentee issues. One manager, Al Wolf, looked out for us since we were both stars on the softball team and he was the team manager. Al was the field supervisor for the repairmen dispatched to businesses or homes in Lower Manhattan. As reported later, he got thirsty one afternoon and dropped into one of the many area bars for a cold one. One turned into a dozen. Rather than bring the New York Telephone van he'd been assigned that day to the garage, he drove it to his West Hempstead, Long Island home–a forbidden thing. Unfortunately, a hit-and-run driver sideswiped the van and badly damaged the passenger side of the vehicle, leaving Al with a dilemma. Sweating bullets, he kept driving and thought up a plan to stay out of trouble. It couldn't have been easy since he was drunk.

A resourceful guy, he decided to turn around, return the van to the company garage, and hope the attendant wouldn't notice the damage. Since it was on the passenger side and the attendant's booth was on the incoming driver's side, Al signed the log, parked the car, and walked up to the Subway station at Chambers Street. He caught the usual series of trains home.

When he was asked about the damage the following morning, he said the van was perfectly fine when he returned it to the garage. Signing the attendant's log was enough evidence to keep him out of trouble. Brilliant!

Through all these adventures, New York Telephone was very good to me. The managers allowed me to work whenever my school schedule allowed. During my senior year at Brooklyn College, I needed nineteen credits to graduate on time. I was an English major with a minor in secondary education. The biggest challenge at college wasn't the coursework: it was the archaic registration process for scheduling classes. I never failed a class, but I did drop one or two along the way. To stay on track, I made up dropped classes during the summers.

Failing out was never an option. The Vietnam war was raging. I had a temporary military draft exemption of 2-S (Student Deferment) and an unlucky low draft lottery number–twenty-two. If my course load dropped or my grades fell below a 2.0 GPA, I would have been drafted and on my way to Vietnam in no time. That's what I call motivation.

During my senior year in 1974, a midnight shift job as a data clerk opened at the Repair Service Bureau. They needed someone to manage computer printer output for a conversion to an electronic switching system. I applied, was accepted, and got an upgrade in pay for the night shift differential.

Three of us were assigned to the midnight shift–Manager Bill Lohan, Tester Bob Salvo, and me. While the shift was serene at times, it also could get boring. The manager was a great guy with only one rule–no sleeping on duty! As the story went, he'd been demoted earlier in his career due to a surprise inspection by a NY Tel executive who found both the manager and tester asleep when they were supposed to be working.

I was allowed to do my homework, read books and magazines, and even have a beer with dinner. I drove to the West Side Diner to grab a beer and a slice of cheesecake. As long as the work got done, I was allowed to do pretty much whatever I wanted–except sleep on duty. Out of sheer boredom one day at 3 a.m., while we all worked in the test bureau, I removed all my clothes and ran around the office, screaming like a lunatic. In 1974 the streaking craze was at its peak. My coworkers looked amazed and terrorized as I ran naked up and down the aisles of the repair service bureau. From that day on, I was called "The Streaker."

The streaker at New York Telephone Company, New York City, 1974

Six college students worked at the West Street Repair Service Bureau throughout that year. They came and went based on school schedules. Some worked part-time hours. Others flexed into a full-time schedule during summer months.

One of them, a Fordham student, was a bit of a character and a serious beer-drinking party boy. His name was Jim Sheridan. He and I had planned to meet one night at the Pig and Whistle Bar in the Bronx near Fordham. We were going to catch a late dinner and have a few beers. Then I was to sleep at his house. His parents were away at the beach for the weekend. Jim told me that if anything happened–if he was late or he missed me at the bar–I should go to his house, locate the spare key, and let myself in.

Sure enough, Jim never showed up at the bar. I went to his house, found the key on the bench under the toolbox, and let myself in. I poured myself a drink from Jim's father's liquor cabinet, stripped to my boxer shorts, and settled in one of the upstairs bedrooms to wait for Jim. I left my near-empty whiskey glass on the nightstand and nodded off. Jim never showed.

The next morning his father, an active FBI agent, rudely awakened me. I opened my bloodshot eyes to see someone aiming a 9mm pistol at my head. He appeared angry and upset to find me in his bed. It was like some weird modern-day Goldilocks story. *Where are my pants?* I thought. *Where are my pants?* Meanwhile, Jim's father kept screaming.

"Who the hell are you?"

"What the hell are you doing here?"

"How did you get in here?"

"What are you? Some kind of long-haired drunk?"

He'd clearly already gone through my wallet so he must have known I worked at the phone company. My photo ID was in the wallet. At 6 a.m. it was already shaping up to be a bad day.

I tried to explain that Jim and I worked together and that he'd invited me to stay over. I fumbled for my pants, socks, and shoes, and put them on while this maniac kept yelling at me. I grabbed my keys and looked for an easy escape from the bedroom. I was sure Mr. Sheridan would physically attack me before I could leave the house. He did not. I drove away quickly, looking in the rearview mirror to be sure the FBI wasn't following me.

Apparently, Jimmy never came home that night, but his father had decided to come home a day early. When I tracked down Jim at work Monday, he laughed the whole thing off.

"My father's a really nice guy," he said, "but he's also sort of a nut."

That was the last time I made plans to hang out with Jimmy.

I kept up my routine, reporting to the phone company at midnight and working until 8:00 a.m. I then hopped in my car and drove to Brooklyn College in Flatbush, listening to *Imus in the Morning* as I crossed the Brooklyn Bridge. That last semester I registered for six courses to get those nineteen credits I needed. After school I drove back to my place in Woodhaven, Queens, not far from South Ozone Park, and tried to sleep. I repeated the process the next day. Sure enough, I passed all my courses with flying colors and went on to graduate in June.

Shortly afterwards, I left the telephone company. It had a hiring/promotion freeze in place and an affirmative action initiative under way that temporarily prevented white males from advancing. Living in my own apartment and wanting to get on with my life, I couldn't wait any longer. I will always appreciate the folks I worked for and with at New York Telephone, though. They were kind and supportive throughout my tenure there.

New York Telephone was partially well known because of its proximity to the original World Trade Center.

When the north tower fell on September 11, 2001, debris piled up against the building all the way up to the seventh floor. Seeing it that way saddened me.

CHAPTER 13

THE SUMMER OF LOVE, 1967

1967-Forever

After my puppy love relationship with Maria ended, I looked for attractive or semi-attractive young ladies with my friends. It wasn't easy. I briefly attracted one very slim and sultry Janice, related somehow to the owner of the local Irish funeral parlor. She had hair like a mannequin, though, and kissed like a three-day-old corpse. I let her pass away.

I transitioned quickly to Dolores, a nice young lady of Italian descent who lived up near St. Anthony's parish. I knew the group of guys she hung around with. My friends and I regularly played rough tackle football against them. Dolores showed the early signs of an emerging moustache, but she was extremely affectionate. She loved Italian food, too. Unfortunately, she may not have heard of mouthwash or deodorant. She had to go.

There were a few more quick flirtations but never anyone with the qualities I was looking for–honesty, trust, compassion, loyalty, intelligence, and a sense of humor. I wanted to meet someone beautiful but humble and, of course, available. It happened in 1967, The Summer of

Love. I met the girl I'd noticed crossing Lefferts Boulevard two years earlier when I was a *Long Island Press* delivery boy. One day she walked by the candy store where I hung out. She had picked up a loaf of Italian bread at Numson's Deli for her family's dinner. She was with her friend Alice, who was always friendly and knew some of my friends.

I learned a few things about the girl. Her name was Carmela. She picked up that bread almost every day. She also had a bad habit: she ate the end of the loaf as she walked home from the store. She switched the wrapper around so her mother wouldn't notice. Clever girl. Carmela's friends from 118th Street and 133rd Avenue knew her as "CeCe." She lived nearby, but CeCe and Alice socialized with a different group of kids, including lots of boys.

Some things I didn't have to ask about. She was beautiful with honey blonde hair, sparkling blue eyes, and the tightest pair of denim shorts a young boy could imagine.

I was intrigued, but there were a couple of problems. First of all, she had sort-of-a-boyfriend named Sal and Sal had a large big brother named Anthony, who was sloth like in a menacing way. Anthony had a unique walk that reminded me of the cartoon character Hardy Har Har. Additionally, Carmela was very shy. How could I get to know her better without triggering an ugly reaction from the boys in her gang, including Sal and Hardy Har Har? Even if I could get past that obstacle, how could I get her to talk to me? She didn't know I was interested or even alive. The girl barely spoke, especially not to boys from the candy store.

As it happened, I found myself spending more and more time riding my bike along Sutter Avenue and up to Alice's house on 118th Street, where the 133rd Avenue girls congregated. They were quite a crew. Alice had a mouth like a sailor on shore leave. Carmela was quiet. Patty was one of nine children and had eight sisters, all of whom seemed to live on Alice's stoop. Alice lived less than half a block from Maria. Carmela lived on Lefferts just around the corner from Alice and Maria.

That neighborhood was a target-rich environment for attractive young women. Within a three-block radius, there were dozens of girls to choose from. There were spoiled brats like Maria, easy girls like Carrie, homely girls like Marylou, short girls like MaryJane, tall girls like Olga, crazy girls like Becky, and one perfect girl in the middle of them all–Carmela.

I guess my interest became obvious since Alice asked me if I "liked" Carmela. Who wouldn't? She was gorgeous. Cute would be an understatement. She had an unusual style about her. She walked with grace and never in a way to attract attention from the neighborhood boys. She didn't seem to flirt and didn't have to be the queen of the hop. She appeared to be ideal and the polar opposite of Maria, who had to be the center of attention at all times.

I'd heard Carmela had a curfew of 10 p.m. in the summer months. I made it a point one night to pass by around 9:45 p.m. I approached her on her way home and asked a series of open-ended questions: "Do you have any brothers or sisters?" "Who does your father work for?" "Is your father a Mets fan or a Yankee fan?" I may have slipped in, "Are you still going out with that funny-looking Sal?"

A day or two later, Sal's big brother firmly suggested that I leave Carmela alone and go back to my own section of the neighborhood. I had just gotten the girl to speak to me and look directly at me for at least fifteen minutes. Not easily intimidated, I was back on Alice's stoop the next day. I believe one of my friends was doodle dashing Alice by flashing his private parts in front of her. She slammed the front door.

Meanwhile, I looked for Carmela to continue our earlier conversation. She was almost always hanging out with Alice or her other good friend Patty with whom she shared a birthday, July 24th. Joe the Ice Cream Man cruised his truck around the neighborhood and gave out free ice cream to anyone celebrating a birthday. Kids lucky enough to have been born in the summer were winners. Those born in the winter missed out. When Carmela and Patty both claimed it was their birthday, Joe looked skeptical. They were both so cute, though, that he came through with a free ice cream pop. He always did.

I learned to rotate among the various groups in the neighborhood. Sometimes I hung out at the candy store. Other times I played poker with the guys on 122nd Street. Occasionally I rode up to the Conduit and spent time with the guys from my football team. I was never one to stay with the same people every day. A diverse group of friends meant a variety of socializing opportunities and lots of options, which appealed to me. If and when trouble started, it also didn't hurt to have a lot of guys to rely on.

I decided to take a chance and ask Carmela to go out with me. She agreed but first politely discarded Sal, as any nice girl would. I wasn't sure why she agreed to go out with me. Fear? Pity? In any case, that was the beginning of a very special friendship. The more I got to know her, the more obvious it became that she was a keeper. While Sal wasn't happy about losing Carmela to a mug from the candy store crowd, he accepted his fate and never caused a problem for us after that summer.

Carmela and I officially started going together on August 10, 1967. I had just turned fifteen. She had just turned fourteen and was starting high school at Stella Maris, Star of the Sea, at the beach in Rockaway, Queens. She had to take the Q10 bus and two subway rides to get to school–a lot of connections, but the public school option, John Adams, was out of the question. Stella Maris was a much better choice. It had an excellent faculty and a fine reputation as one of the more desirable all-girls Catholic high schools in the city.

That September I started my sophomore year at Bishop Loughlin. My commute was a bus and single subway ride through some of Brooklyn's most dangerous neighborhoods, which were racially charged and rampant with crime. The school was excellent but the neighborhood, Bedford Stuyvesant, not so much. The Bishop Loughlin principal was Brother Baldwin Peter, a Christian brother who became a friend through my involvement in the Student Council and National Honor Society.

Unlike my previous girlfriend's parents, who frowned upon her having a boyfriend at such an early age, Carmela's parents didn't mind. They welcomed me into their home and treated me like an honored guest. I'm sure they didn't think the relationship would last more than fifty years and, after all, they knew my brother was a priest.

Tommy adopted by Carmela's family.

Carmela and I did our homework together in her kitchen and listened to albums by the Beatles, Young Rascals, and the Beach Boys. We sat on the front stoop for hours talking about nothing and everything. We waited for her parents to call her inside at which point I kissed her good night. Sometimes we walked around the corner to Alice's house and watched *Superman* reruns in the basement. We had fun doing simple things with the rest of the kids in the neighborhood, too.

That summer we had our first real date at Shea Stadium. The game got rained out early so we left, which was unfortunate. I'd paid $1.60 each for those nosebleed seats even though it was customary to sneak down to the field level as the game went along. I extended the date by taking Carmela to Kennedy Airport on the bus even though the fare cost me an additional fifteen cents each. This dating business was getting expensive.

Kennedy Airport was fascinating, though. We walked around the terminals, making fun at the foreigners and riding up and down the elevator at the air traffic controller building until they kicked us out. We also visited Our Lady of the Skies Chapel, where we lit candles for a dime and prayed for the Mets.

Future dates included Jahn's Ice Cream Parlor, which featured everything from ice cream sundaes to the "Kitchen Sink," which had almost enough ice cream cherries and syrup to feed an army or perhaps our buddy, Fat Ralph. We went to the Hillside Roller Rink or Americana Lanes to bowl. When funds were really low Carmela slid onto the front part of my bicycle and I pedaled us down to the Conduit park or up to Liberty Avenue.

Three movie theaters were within striking distance. The Lefferts and the dingy Casino were on Liberty Avenue. The third was the Crossbay, which required taking the Q7 rather than the more reliable Q10 but was reachable if the other two didn't have anything good to see. The Crossbay had an added attraction–a White Castle across the street where we bought fifteen-cent hamburgers by the sack. I took Carmela to see *To Sir, with Love*, starring

Sydney Poitier in 1967 when it opened and Lulu had the No. 1 song by the same name on AM radio.

From the very beginning, there were no arguments, no temper tantrums, and no flirting with other boys. Money was always a minor issue, but Carmela didn't ask for much and we got by on what I made at Rizzo's Restaurant on 101st Avenue and Lefferts Boulevard. One of my brother Vic's friends, a nun, knew the owners. By that time my parents had separated, the Brooklyn Navy Yard had closed, and my father had relocated to Pennsylvania for a job at the Philadelphia Navy Yard. My mother didn't work but often volunteered at the rectory, so money was always tight.

I wanted extra spending cash but wouldn't ask my mother for money I knew she didn't have. Once I asked her for five dollars so I could accompany friends to the World's Fair in Flushing.

"I don't have five dollars to my name," she confessed. "Why don't you return empty soda bottles to the A&P supermarket? They redeem them for five cents a bottle."

I did. It took several trips and I never forgot that experience. I knew I had to get some kind of job.

Two brothers, Joe and Frank, owned and operated Rizzo's. They alternated hours, cooked the food, and ran the table service. There were roughly fifteen tables, a small bar, and a jukebox filled with Frank Sinatra and Jerry Vale records. The starting and ending pay for a busboy was a dollar an hour. Though I was the busboy, I also washed dishes if the regular guy, Richie, didn't show up. He frequently didn't show up. In addition to my one-dollar-per-hour wage, the waitresses occasionally threw me two or three bucks from their share of tips. There was one perk: if I worked at least five hours, I was entitled to a free dinner–and the food was great.

The job required normal busboy tasks–setting tables, clearing tables, running drinks or food, and making extra pizza boxes. At the night's end, I was also expected to clean the bathrooms, mop the floors, and put up all the chairs. They had me fill small bottles of wine from much larger bottles to maximize profits. Nothing went to waste.

I probably wasn't the best busboy in the world as I'd rarely been to a restaurant as a child. I tried hard, though, and became better over time. At the end of a shift my clothes smelled like garlic and onions. I hated that. Every night I had to wash the odor of the special of the day out of my hair.

As I rode the bus home after work one day, I calculated how much money I could make by the end of summer. It wasn't enough to buy a used bike and a new peacoat. One Sunday afternoon, the waitress called in sick. Joe asked me to fill in as the waiter. *Wow! A promotion.* As it happened, the uncle of one of my friends from 115th Street came for an early dinner. He handed me a five-dollar tip on the way out. Best tip ever. Rather than putting it in the tip jar, I slipped it into my shirt pocket. It was a good thing I did, too. At the end of the night, Joe, one of the owners, rather than thanking me for working as both waiter and busboy, gave me half the tips and pocketed the rest for himself. Nice guy, huh? On the other hand, the brothers never found out I was passing jugs of wine over the back fence to my friends as I threw out the garbage. Or that I munched on meatballs every time I passed through the kitchen. Both sort of made up for the low wages and cranky bosses.

A week or so later, the dishwasher, Richie, didn't show up. Frank, the other owner, assigned me to be the dishwasher. The regular waitress was really slow. When food was ready to be served, the brothers rang a bell to alert the waitress. Overwhelmed with mountains of dirty dishes at the time, I struggled to get enough glasses cleaned to keep the customers happy. Frank rang the bell once, twice, a third time. No waitress. I sensed his frustration. The food was getting colder by the minute.

Trying to be helpful, I reached over and rang the bell a fourth time. He got mad.

"You drop what you're doing and serve the food!" he said.

I was filthy and wet from washing dishes and didn't think it was fair to expect me to do both jobs, especially for a dollar an hour. I quit on the spot. The next afternoon I returned to collect my final seven dollars in pay, which one brother reluctantly forked over.

At one point, to make a few extra bucks, I simultaneously worked at two different messenger services on Wall Street. From there I went to KFC and took a part-time manager's position after school in Woodside for the *Long Island Press*. Because of my experiences working these low-paying dead-end jobs, I began to understand and appreciate the value of a good college education.

Tom and Carmela at Bishop Loughlin senior prom, 1970, in New York City.

My relationship with Carmela blossomed through the years. Our first date at Shea Stadium evolved into going steady and an ankle bracelet, which certainly didn't come from Plaid Land. She graduated from Stella Maris in 1971. After we both graduated from college, she with a bachelor's degree in Elementary Education at Richmond College, CUNY, we found full-time jobs and got engaged.

We made a concerted effort to go about life doing the right things in the right sequence. I invited Carmela's father, Joe, to meet me at the Locust Grove bar on Lefferts Boulevard to ask for his blessing. I wanted to propose to Carmela. He was relieved when I asked him. I'd never before suggested that we meet in a bar. I'm sure the reason for the invitation concerned him.

Carmela and I married in 1977. A photo in our wedding album shows her dancing with her 104-year-old grandfather, Rosario, at the reception. Rosario, a legend in the neighborhood, lived with Carmela's Aunt Mary next door in Queens. Rosario Provenzano came to America in 1895 while in his twenties. A shoemaker, he worked for many years as a footwear crafter in a Brooklyn factory with other Italian immigrants. He never felt the need to master English. After almost ninety years in America, he still proudly stuck to his native Calabrese dialect. He passed at the age of 108. The joke at the time was that if his bungee cord hadn't snapped, he would have lived to 200.

Carmela and I left the old neighborhood in 1980 when we purchased our first home in North Valley Stream, Long Island for the seemingly enormous sum of fifty-five thousand dollars. We stayed almost eight years and then moved to Massapequa, Long Island, home of the infamous Buttafuoco clan, where we lived another six years. We bought that house for one hundred fifty thousand dollars and sold it for two hundred fifty thousand dollars in 1993 when we moved to beautiful Bucks County, Pennsylvania. We stumbled upon Doylestown, Pennsylvania in a corporate relocation investigation. Ever since we've enjoyed a higher quality of life and much lower cost of living. Long Island was great, but the taxes, utilities, and traffic were killing us.

Carmela dancing with her 104-year-old grandfather at 1977 wedding reception in Queens, New York.

Like her grandfather, Carmela is a celebrity of sorts around town. Since we moved to town, she's taught nearly one thousand kindergarten students at the local Catholic school, Our Lady of Mount Carmel, five minutes from our home. Carmela has always had a special gift for communicating with children of all ages, a trait she passed on to our son. Both Carmela and TJ are school-teachers and make a difference for so many kids every day. Both TJ, his wife Jessica, and our daughter, Juliet, lead successful, productive lives and own their own homes a half hour from us.

No doubt growing up in Brooklyn and Queens was invaluable to me later in life. Those experiences–the good, the bad, and the ugly–forged me into the person I am today. Carmela and I love reuniting with our friends from Queens, who are scattered all over the map. While some don't remember old times as fondly as we do, most are happy to celebrate our youth. We find the time to gather with Billy, Mooch, Sanzi, Pat, Debbie, Pam, Alice, Joe, Johnny D, Audrey, Patty, and Abe in Doylestown, Manhattan, and Long Island. Hopefully, some of our other long-lost friends will join us in the future. No one knows how many more opportunities we'll have to tell the old stories and share a few hugs and laughs.

Why not? After all, Rizzo's Ristorante is still offering the early bird menu for people our age.

Epilogue

N one of us knows how things are going to work out in life. That's what keeps it interesting. The run-down, crumbling neighborhoods where we grew up in Bushwick, East New York, and Bed-Stuy in Brooklyn have enjoyed a revival. Some of those six-family tene-ments have been remodeled, with many of the brown-stones selling for a million dollars or more.

Similarly, the neighborhoods in South Ozone Park and Richmond Hill, which had become sketchy due to a migration of lower-income people from areas west of the Van Wyck Expressway near Jamaica, have also seen a surprising rebirth. These sections of Queens, which re-main a melting pot of cultures, have become sought-after destinations for peace-loving Asians, Guyanese, Koreans, Chinese, Indians, Pakistanis, and Haitians, among others.

The empty lots on Sutter Avenue and 122nd Street are now filled with homes. But when I look at them I remem-ber Billy Hawk, Frankie D, and I playing blackjack in the night watchman's trailer next to the abandoned mansion with the empty plaster pool. John Blades, where we for-merly bought raw peas for our peashooter wars, is long gone. Change doesn't just happen. As we get older, it ac-celerates.

As I look back over the past six-and-a-half decades, I consider myself very fortunate. I write this epilogue while sipping a hot cup of organic tea at my favorite hangout in town, The Doylestown Bookshop. It's a beautiful day in a beautiful place!

Getting to this point with great harmony has been quite a journey. I have held many jobs along the way to fund the trip. I've been a *Long Island Press* paper boy, Wall Street messenger, drug store delivery boy, busboy, waiter, cashier, dishwasher, fast food counter person, gas station attendant, clerk, searcher, box folder, customer service manager, sales representative, trainer, recruiter, sales executive, Karate studio owner, husband, and father. The last two were the best.

I've made and lost a lot of friends along the way. My best friend remains my beautiful wife, Carmela, who patiently puts up with my sick humor, sarcasm, and brooding Irish moods. Without her pleasant outlook and sense of humor, it would have been impossible to stick together for fifty-one years. And if she hadn't typed all my term papers and student council election speeches at Bishop Loughlin, Brooklyn College, and LIU Grad School, I may never even have completed the education that prepared me for long, successful careers at UARCO and Staples Business Advantage.

Given where we started, few would have predicted how far we've come.

While we've been blessed with great family moral support and encouragement, neither of us enjoyed significant family financial support. We literally had to open a few envelopes during our wedding reception at the Royal Manor Catering Hall to pay the reception bill. When we moved into our first house in Valley Stream, we had thirty-five dollars left in our savings account. Somehow, we got by.

I consider myself very lucky to have had the family I had growing up. My brother Victor has been an inspiration and role model my entire life. My brother Dan and my sister Ginger and brother-in-law Tony, who took me in when my mother passed away, are no longer with us but will never be forgotten.

I am also blessed to have friends from all eras of my life and to live in Doylestown, where life is good and the softball team I play for has won the Bucks County Senior League championship for the last five years. Of course, our Friday softball practices and beer meetings at the Penn Tap Room are weekly highlights during the warmer months. Rich and Brian both accompanied me last January to a softball tournament in Tampa, Florida. If the Mets had a team like us with great players like Rich, Brian, Rob, Barry, Keith, and Tim, they would likely be nearly unbeatable.

Great friends make life easier. Carmela and I always look forward to our dinners, concerts, and backyard pool parties and barbecues with our good local friends Brian and Ronnie and Rich and Diane. These are special people. No matter what breaks in our house or on our cars, either Brian or Rich or both know how to fix the problem. They are always available to help out and never fail to come prepared.

My good friend Rich Hansen, formerly of Hancock Street in Brooklyn, wound up living the good life in Bucks County, too. In 2015 we returned to the old Bushwick neighborhood for a good will tour. Little did he know I'd brought along a sawed-off broom handle and a Spalding rubber ball. As we turned the corner of Evergreen and Putnam avenues, I pulled the car over, opened the trunk, and pulled out the stickball equipment.

Rich was almost as stunned as the three locals watching us from a stoop. I asked him to play the field (in the middle of Putnam Avenue) and proceeded to hit him a few line drives. After a few too many sewer shots, I handed the bat to Rich and played the field. I invited the locals to join us in the middle of the street, but they declined. They told me they'd never played stickball and watched our game closely.

Glenda and Alan, who own The Doylestown Book-shop, are great people, too. So is Daniel, the manager, and the staff—Nathan, Hannah, Krisy, Brett, Meredith, Lisa, Peter, Pamela, and Jennifer. They all make that store a special place. Sue and Shawn, bookstore employees, and the rest of the gang have become good friends and occasionally visit in the summer for pool parties and barbecues.

Tom and Carmela's wedding day, August 27, 1977, with Carmela's parents, Joe and Jean Provenzano.

I look back to that folded paper stoop game we used to play on Sutter Avenue. It was a game of fortune. Girls wrote down future random life circumstances on cleverly folded pieces of paper. They wrote things like how many children you might have, or what kind of house or car you'd buy, or how many times you'd get married. Each of us picked a corner and read the future to the others. All my future hopes and wishes have come true. It wasn't always perfect, but I can't complain. Life is good. How lucky can you get?

As my friend Bob Ramirez used to say, "Think happy thoughts!"

Now if only the Mets could play like it's 1986 and win the World Series again.

Carmela and Tom Herbert in 2018.

Acknowledgments

Remembering the details of events that took place fifty years ago can be challenging. I apologize in advance for omitting anyone who made the experience memorable.

I start by thanking my beautiful wife of forty-two years, Carmela. She has provided an incredible amount of happiness and inspiration through the years, beginning in 1967 when we formally met. Her sense of humor, intelligence, and loyalty have been invaluable.

My children, TJ and Juliet, have been supportive and helpful. Both have heard the stories throughout their lives and encouraged me to write them so others could enjoy and cherish them as we have.

Great friends like Billy and Mooch made this book possible by living interesting lives and providing an endless source of content and memories. While I shared advance copies of the book with both, neither has seen the final draft. I hope they fully enjoy the finished product.

Special thanks to my editor, Lorraine Ash, for walking me patiently through the process and minimizing my tendencies to jump around in the story.

I decided to write the book after reading *Jefferson Avenue: Stories from a Brooklyn Boyhood 1941-1958,* by

James M. O'Kane. Jim, who grew up in Bushwick, was a family friend who went on to have a successful career as a college professor at Drew University. Thanks to Jim for encouragement and guidance.

Friends such as Daniel, Brian, and Rich also took the time to offer suggestions along the way. To them, I am eternally grateful.

Additionally, I thank my brother, Victor Herbert, who inspired and encouraged both me and Carmela to go to college and get a quality education, which has allowed us to live the wonderful lives we have enjoyed.

About the Author

From his "poor and lucky" beginnings in Brooklyn and Queens, Tom Herbert went on to study English at Brooklyn College. Inspired in part by his teachers at Bishop Loughlin Memorial High School, he graduated in 1974 with the goal of becoming a high school English teacher.

The scarcity of teaching jobs led Tom to the business world. In 1975 he began work as a customer service manager at a Long Island City-based linens and yarn manufacturing company.

Three years later, newly married, Tom joined UARCO as a sales representative. He worked his way up the ranks and was area vice president for the eastern half of the United States when UARCO went out of business in 1997.

Tom was recruited to Staples immediately after leaving UARCO and is now director of field sales for their Corporate Strategic Accounts Division.

Even after forty-five years in business, Tom's love of English still shows, both in *Growing Up Poor and Lucky in New York City*, his first book, and in the copy of Walt Whitman's *Leaves of Grass* that he keeps on his nightstand.

Tom Herbert with his beloved pup, Madison.

Herbert has been a lifelong martial artist and along with his son, TJ, owned and operated a karate dojo in Bucks County for many years. In addition to his black belt passion, Tom continues to actively participate in Senior League competitive softball.

Tom lives in Doylestown, Pennsylvania with his wife of 42 years, Carmela, and his dog, Madison Marie. His children, TJ and Juliet, are grown and live nearby.

The Herbert home in Doylestown (Bucks County), Pennsylvania.

TJ, Tom, Carmela, and Juliet Herbert.

TJ and Jessica Herbert with Tom and Carmela's first grandchild, Connor Joseph, October 2019.

TJ, Tom, and Jess Herbert celebrating Bucks County senior men's softball championship, 2018.

Carmela and Juliet Herbert at TJ and Jessica's wedding in July of 2017.

CPSIA information can be obtained
at www.ICGtesting.com
Printed in the USA
LVHW042207251119
638498LV00005B/569/P

9 780578 604008